Power and
Organization Development

Power and Organization Development

Mobilizing Power to Implement Change

Larry E. Greiner
University of Southern California

Virginia E. Schein
Gettysburg College

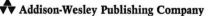 **Addison-Wesley Publishing Company**
Reading, Massachusetts • Menlo Park, California • New York • Don Mills, Ontario •
Wokingham, England • Amsterdam • Bonn • Sydney • Singapore • Tokyo •
Madrid • San Juan

This book is in the Addison-Wesley Series on Organization Development.
Editors: Edgar H. Schein, Richard Beckhard

Other titles in the series:

Organizational Transitions:
Managing Complex Change, Second
Edition
Richard Beckhard and Reuben Harris

Organization Development:
A Normative View
W. Warner Burke

Team Building:
Issues and Alternatives, Second
Edition
William G. Dyer

The Technology Connection:
Strategy and Change in the
Information Age
Marc S. Gerstein

Designing Organizations for High
Performance
David P. Hanna

Stream Analysis:
A Powerful Way to Diagnose and
Manage Organizational Change
Jerry I. Porras

Process Consultation, Volume I: Its
Role in Organization Development,
Second Edition
Edgar H. Schein

Process Consultation Volume II:
Lessons for Managers and
Consultants
Edgar H. Schein

Managing Conflict:
Interpersonal Dialogue and Third-
Party Roles,
Second Edition
Richard E. Walton

Library of Congress Cataloging-in-Publication Data

Greiner, Larry E.
  Power and organization development.

  (Addison-Wesley OD series)
  Bibliography: p.
  1. Organizational change. 2. Power (Social
sciences) I. Schein, Virginia E. II. Title.
III. Series: Addison-Wesley series on organization
development.
HD58.8.G73 1988   658.4′063   87–24124
ISBN 0–201–12185–9

Reprinted with corrections, March 1989.

CDEFGHIJ–BA–89

We dedicate this book to our children
From Larry to Corinne and Justine
and
From Virginia to Alexander

Foreword

The Addison-Wesley Series on Organization Development originated in the late 1960s when a number of us recognized that the rapidly growing field of "OD" was not well understood or well defined. We also recognized that there was no one OD philosophy, and hence one could not at that time write a textbook on the theory and practice of OD, but one could make clear what various practitioners were doing under that label. So the original six books by Beckhard, Bennis, Blake and Mouton, Lawrence and Lorsch, Schein, and Walton launched what has since become a continuing enterprise. The essence of this enterprise was to let different authors speak for themselves instead of trying to summarize under one umbrella what was obviously a rapidly growing and highly diverse field.

By 1981 the series included nineteen titles, having added books by Beckhard and Harris, Cohen and Gadon, Davis, Dyer, Galbraith, Hackman and Oldham, Heenan and Perlmutter, Kotter, Lawler, Nadler, Roeber, Schein, and Steele. This proliferation reflected what had happened to the field of OD. It was growing by leaps and bounds, and it was expanding into all kinds of organizational areas and technologies of intervention. By this time many textbooks existed as well that tried to capture the core concepts of the field, but we felt that diversity and innovation were still the more salient aspects of OD today.

The present series is an attempt both to recapture some basics and to honor the growing diversity. So we have begun a series of revisions of some of the original books and have added a set of new authors or old authors with new content. Our hope is to capture the spirit of inquiry and innovation that has always been the hallmark of organization development and to launch with these books a new wave of insights into the forever tricky problem of how to change and improve organizations.

We are grateful that Addison-Wesley has chosen to continue the series and are also grateful to the many reviewers who have helped us and the authors in the preparation of the current series of books.

Cambridge, Massachusetts   Edgar H. Schein
New York, New York   Richard Beckhard

Preface

Our hope is to reach two audiences with this book: primarily, we are addressing the OD practitioners and students of OD, many of whom idealistically espouse a more humane world of work without understanding the political realities involved; but we also speak to the practicing manager who frequently is more comfortable with power and politics while overlooking human potential in contributing to positive outcomes.

For too long, we believe, power and OD have been distinguished as two opposing and contentious approaches to management. Our theme is different: we argue that OD and power can and should integrate themselves better in the implementation of change. Both schools of thought need one another to compensate for the limits of each. Together they can exert a more potent impact in dealing with vital concerns of social adaptation in organizations today and into the future.

The writing of this book has been an enjoyable ordeal. We have few others to thank except ourselves for putting up with petty fights that turned into laughter and insights, or cajoling one another to make deadlines that became cause for relief and celebration. Ed Schein (no relation) gave us the valuable feedback that we expected and needed on an earlier draft; he was tough, correct, and caring. Arvind Bhambri provided research and insight for the Mega Corporation case study. Ronald Festa worked extensively

on the power strategies research. Nancy Benjamin provided in-
valuable editorial assistance. And our two mates at home performed admirably—Larry's wife, Marta, with understanding and
overtime on the copying machine, and Virginia's son, Alexander,
with schoolwork and ball games to relieve monotony in front of
the computer.

Along the way, we decided to include two original empirical pieces of research that have not been published elsewhere:
Virginia Schein's study of managerial power strategies, and Larry
Greiner's case analysis of strategic change at the Mega Corporation. We believe these two studies enliven the book and contribute useful knowledge to the literature on power and OD. To the
anonymous and sharing participants in these studies, we are
deeply grateful.

Palos Verdes, California   L.E.G.
Gettysburg, Pennsylvania   V.E.S.

Contents

Power and
Organization Development

1

Reconciling Power with OD

OD and power appear as odd bedfellows in the recent history of management thought and practice. Advocates of OD argue for an enlightenment process, using re-education techniques to free employees from unconscious and destructive forces (the "hidden agenda") existing within organizations and people. By unleashing human potential, OD seeks to create new opportunities and resources never before envisioned by the leaders of impersonal bureaucratic structures.

Competing with this humanistic point of view are the scholars and practitioners of a political view of management. They stress the inevitability of vested-interest groups within organizations fighting over scarce resources. Moreover, individuals are seen as acting from a base of self-interest to pursue positions of control, status, and reward. A process of bargaining and compromise results in winners and losers.

It is little wonder that these two camps have rarely communicated effectively with each other in the past. OD, from its infancy in the late 1950s, became the enemy of the entrenched power structure by pressing it to open up and change. Power enthusiasts, on the other hand, ridiculed OD for adhering to an idealistic and therefore seriously mistaken view of human nature and decision-making in organizations.

If one confronts these two diverse views of organizational life, a paralyzing choice is presented. Does one join with OD and the forces for "good over evil," or does one accept the "real world" and learn to live pragmatically with the imperfections of humans and the inherent limits of organizations?

To choose one point of view over the other can lead to unfortunate consequences for both the humanists and politicians. Mirvis and Berg, in their controversial book *Failures in Organization Development and Change* (1977), chronicle numerous OD efforts that fell by the wayside because of neglect and lack of support by top management. We know one Fortune 100 company that abandoned a major OD program because a senior executive learned on the tennis court about an OD sponsored interracial confrontation meeting in the company. This kind of incident can prompt the power advocates to proclaim gleefully, "I told you so."

Yet the demise of once proud Lehman Brothers points clearly to the destructive forces inherent in power and politics (Auletta, 1986). In that case, the greedy side of self-interest destroyed a successful firm and forced its sale to Shearson-American Express.

Uneasy Coexistence

Recent years have seen gradual movement away from the standoff that the above polarity implies. The birth of matrix organizations signaled a move away from steep pyramids toward decentralized teams of highly skilled and interdependent workers. Powerful leaders of these avant-garde organizations, such as Reuben Mettler of TRW, supported OD as a means for making their organizations work better.

In addition, OD zealots learned to temper their language with talk of the bottom line. Some ODers even made peace with Theory X executives who were willing to back their efforts. Many OD change agents displayed a willingness to utilize techniques that previously had been labeled by OD as authoritarian, such as behavior modification and assessment centers. Still others decided to go underground by disguising OD with new titles, such as "Organization Effectiveness."

These alliances and subterfuges were spawned by an end justifies the means rationale. A few key executives with power recognized that OD, if closely controlled, could be used to achieve business objectives. And OD pragmatists, looking out for their survival, proved willing to listen, compromise, and even conform.

The net result, by the late 1970s in many organizations, was that power and OD had moved into the same house, though often in separate bedrooms. The 1960s brand of revolutionary OD had given way to a new eclecticism. If a new plant could be designed using sociotechnical theory, with team building thrown in, then that was called OD. Or if action research could be used to eliminate a turnover problem, then OD assumed a scientific guise in its administration of questionnaires and the feedback of quantitative data.

Nevertheless, critics of this transition began to ask if OD had lost its soul by selling out to the power elite (Greiner, 1980). In OD's quest for survival, had it forgotten its humanistic origins, only to become the servant of power? More pointedly, had the early advocates of the power school actually won out?

Your Resolution of the Dual Forces

We think it useful to pause at this initial stage in the book to see how you personally may have weathered this historical tug of war between OD and power. Here we suggest that you fill out your responses to the eight questions listed below. It is a forced choice questionnaire, so select the *one* statement in each pair that best represents your preferred approach to introducing change into organizations.

I prefer a change approach that . . .

1. _____ tries to motivate people to change the situation around them.
   _____ helps people to adjust better to the situation facing them.

2. _____ emphasizes the need for a total system change from one organizational state to another.

_____ introduces changes that are geared more to making the existing situation work better.

3. _____ provides new value alternatives, such as collaboration, confrontation, etc.

_____ works to solve practical problems facing people in the organization.

4. _____ strives for significant change introduced through a planned program over one to two years.

_____ moves ahead step by step toward gradual change over several years.

5. _____ works closely with lower and middle level employees in helping to improve the organization above and around them.

_____ works closely with top management in helping to improve the organization below them.

6. _____ provides strong leadership to move others toward a plan and method of change.

_____ brings others together so they may develop their ideas into a plan and method of change.

7. _____ seeks better and more effective behavioral relationships between employees.

_____ strives for greater productivity and motivation from employees.

8. _____ helps to bring out the potential in people and organizations to achieve beyond their expectations.

_____ recognizes and accepts the practical limits in available resources within organizations.

Now you can score it yourself. Add up all your first blank checks to get a total score, and then do the same for the second blank checks. The questionnaire is constructed so that the answers next to all of the first blanks take a more revolutionary stance toward change—that is, the goal is large-scale change to advance human values. Answers next to the second blanks speak more to pragamatism, emphasizing gradualism, short-term results, and attention to the values of those in power.

If your total score is 8 in the first blanks and 0 in the second blanks, you still adhere closely to the original concept of OD as a revolutionary and humanistic force. Conversely, if your score is 8 to 0 in favor of the second blanks, you have probably become a "servant of power." A score somewhere in between represents an accommodation or compromise between both points of view.

When we have given this questionnaire to others, line managers tend to report the highest scores toward power and pragmatism, followed by internal staff people in consulting roles. High scorers in revolutionary approaches and idealism tend to work outside business corporations, acting more as consultants to non-profit organizations, as trainers in public workshops, or as academics in universities.

Letting Go of the Past

Our focus in this book aims for a deeper and more integrated perspective in which OD and power become closely interwoven. Simplistic notions that power only resides at the top, or that lower level employees are powerless, must give way to more contemporary and complex notions of power. The antipower rhetoric of traditional OD, such as Theory X is bad and Theory Y is good, are amusing anachronisms. Such cornerstone ideas of the old OD as *power redistribution* and *bottoms-up change* can prove unworkable in times of industry turmoil and organization crisis.

A more contemporary viewpoint reveals power to be a diffuse and elusive reality in modern organizations, residing perhaps in the R&D department, the labor union, or a disgruntled consumer group. Often, top management is only a vague term for the office of the president or a matrix of leaders spread over the world. Furthermore, the OD group itself may possess more or less power in a rapidly shifting interpretation of what is meant by *human resources management*.

This is not to say that power in organizations has become so diffuse and fleeting that it is irrelevant. Quite the contrary, it is very much alive—if one abandons narrow hierarchical and formal notions of power—and recognizes that it can be summed up as one's capacity to get others to do what one wants them to do. As we shall see, power is derived from a multiplicity of factors, including one's reputation and social network. It is also exercised in a variety of ways, ranging from a forthright presentation of data to outright deception.

Issues of concern to key powerholders at the top of organizations have also changed dramatically during the 1980s. Change has become a constant in the turbulent economy of deregulation and global competition. Huge growth in the service sector is largely dependent on people and not machines. Shorter product life cycles require rapid innovation and intense coordination across departmental boundaries. Unfriendly takeovers represent a constant threat to underperforming companies with ill prepared strategic plans. Political action groups lay in wait for companies that stumble in their conduct and treatment of multiple stakeholders.

While these new conditions appear favorable for the application of OD, we have not seen much evidence that OD is prepared to assist key powerholders in resolving them. Not only do OD's techniques of team building and interpersonal feedback seem outdated but even more troubling is its weak power base for exercising influence. In many organizations OD remains naive in recognizing power, acquiring it, and using it effectively. As a result, senior managements do not call upon OD when they face difficult challenges. Whether a powerless OD will be left behind in these changing times is its most pressing agenda.

Our Purpose

It is the enlightened use of power by OD that we are most concerned with as the subject of this book. Our position is that OD has much to offer and, in fact, must offer to assist organizations and their employees in coping with Naisbitt's *Megatrends* (1982) or Peters's *Passion for Excellence* (1986). Our worry is that OD will not adapt fast enough to incorporate contemporary uses of power to assert influence.

The effective combination of OD and power represents, for us, taking the *high road* to organization improvement. It begins by adhering to the valuable roots of OD where an educational process is used to encourage people to collaborate in making decisions that affect their own destiny. But, as we will attempt to show in this book, OD goes on to incorporate modern approaches to power by (1) building its own power base so that it has access to those in power, (2) utilizing power strategies that are open and above-board for influencing key powerholders to accept the use of OD, (3) providing a facilitative process for these powerholders to address critical substantive issues that proves more creative and efficient than political bargaining, (4) assisting the power structure to confront and transform itself so that change can be more lasting, and (5) upholding the concerns and interests of those with less power who are affected by these changes.

The *low road* represents vested political interest groups who, if left only to power and deception without OD, can destroy organizations by failing to tap human potential. Ironically, the *low road* also includes not only traditional champions of power who think that manipulation and political games are the essence of success, but those OD chameleons who sell out to power.

Even if we concede that taking the *low road* can sometimes achieve certain desirable ends, such as higher short-term profits, we clearly prefer the higher path that preserves and furthers the dignity of people in the decision making process. Our hope is that the *new* OD will make this same choice, knowing that power and OD are not incompatible if used constructively and responsibly.

This book is divided into two major parts: Part I—*Power and the Practicing Manager*, and Part II—*The Integration of Power with OD*. In Part I, Chapters 2–6, the OD consultant enters into the realm of organizational reality where power, from the manager's point of view, is considered essential for getting things done.

Chapter 2, *Defining a Political Model of Organizations*, examines three models of organizational functioning—Bureaucratic/Rational, Collegial/Consensus, and Pluralistic/Political to show how one's model in use of organizations affects our attitudes, understanding, and treatment of power.

Chapter 3, *Developing Power Bases*, identifies those individual and departmental resources that provide managers with a platform from which to exercise power. Eleven different power bases are described, each of which makes a significant difference in a manager's degree of influence.

Next, in Chapter 4, *Using Power Strategies*, we see how managers develop and use a range of influence strategies built from their respective power bases. Based upon research from over three hundred managers, eighteen different power strategies are identified, and these strategies are divided into more and less successful approaches.

Chapters 5 and 6 explore the more subjective, sometimes unpleasant, aspects of power. In Chapter 5, *Deceiving Others Through Power: All That Glitters . . .* , both the negative and positive sides of political intrigue are considered. Chapter 6, *Personalizing Power*, looks at how an individual's background and personality contribute to one's power style and its use for constructive and destructive outcomes.

Part II, Chapters 7–12, builds upon this foundation of knowledge about power to demonstrate how OD and power can join together to create major strategic and organizational change. Chapter 7, *Diagnosing Power*, discusses specific data gathering techniques for the OD consultant to use in uncovering how power exists and is played out in organizations.

Chapter 8, *Mega Corporation Stage I: Consolidating Power to Prepare for Change*, gives an indepth description of a situation in which an OD consultant assists the top management of a major corporation to begin a change effort that will eventually transform the company. Chapters 9, 10, and 11 make extensive reference to the Mega case.

Stage II: Focusing Power on Strategic Consensus is addressed in Chapter 9, in which we consider how OD is used at Mega to develop and identify strategic alternatives to bring about eventual agreement to a divided top management group on a new strategic direction.

Chapter 10, *Stage III: Aligning Power with Structure and People*, describes the use of OD to design an organization structure to fit Mega's new strategy, and then to place the right people in the right jobs. In essence, the power structure at Mega transforms itself.

In Chapter 11, *Stage IV: Releasing Power Through Leadership and Collaboration,* we see the dramatic results of Mega's change effort as many employees respond with greater motivation and effectiveness. The chapter identifies those conditions at Mega, as well as in other situations, where OD may or may not find a common ground with power to produce significant change.

Chapter 12, *Acquiring and Using Power as a Change Agent,* concludes and reflects on the practical and ethical problems of an OD consultant in building a power base and using power responsibly to influence others.

Part I
Power and the Practicing Manager

2

Defining a Political Model of Organizations

Power is a complex and ambiguous concept, which has been tossed about and examined by social theorists since ancient times. Some scholars define power in terms of its sources, while others focus on its intended outcomes. All definitions seem to be concerned with the exercise of social influence to fill some need or meet some goal. However, for us to review the specifics of all these definitions of power in search of one final definition serves only to move us farther away from understanding the concrete and practical dynamics of power in organizations. We choose, therefore, not to sink into definitional quicksand; instead, our view of power is simple, workable, and goes to the heart of what power is about.

Power is the capacity to influence another person or group to accept one's own ideas or plans. In essence, power enables you to get others to do what you want them to do.

It is the *who, what, when,* and *where* of power that makes understanding and dealing with power so complex and challenging. Power is multifaceted and dynamic when it comes into play; there are many potential sources of power and a variety of ways to express it. Moreover, the outcomes are far from certain because other people have power too. Also, power can be subtle, reflected in the fact that people with a great deal of power may rarely exercise it, because others anticipate the wishes of the powerholder.

This chapter begins by considering three basic directions for expressing power in organizations—downward, upward, and sideways. We then compare how these directions are commonly considered under three alternative models of organizational behavior. Whether we highlight or ignore a particular expression of power relates to our implicit model for understanding behavior in organizations. If, for example, we adhere to a participative model, we are likely to abhor autocratic practices. Or if we prefer organic matrix models, we become frustrated with rigid bureaucracies.

Power Directions

The most commonly considered expression of power in organization research and practice is *downward* power, which is the influence of a superior over a subordinate. This kind of influence in the form of one having power over another is a central focus in much of our traditional leadership research and training, such as Theory X versus Theory Y or task oriented versus people oriented styles.

Upward power refers to attempts by subordinates to influence their superiors. Until recently, subordinates were considered relatively powerless. But a small and growing body of research indicates that subordinates can and do influence their superiors in subtle ways. Studies by Kipnis, Schmidt, and Wilkinson (1980) and Schlilit and Locke (1982) have identified subordinate influence strategies such as persistence, logical presentation of ideas, coalition formation, and ingratiation. And Gabarro and Kotter (1980) have argued that the leadership challenge for most subordinates is to learn how to manage one's boss.

A third direction, *sideways* power, refers to influence attempts directed at those people who are neither subordinates nor superiors in one's immediate reporting chain of authority. *Horizontal power, interdepartmental power, external relationships,* and *lateral relationships* are all terms that reflect expressions of sideways power. Various researchers have called attention to this increasingly important expression of power in organizations—Mintzberg, 1973; Strauss, 1962, at the individual level and Hickson et al., 1971; Pfeffer and Salancik, 1974, at the subunit level.

Interestingly, the net result of these research studies has been to show that sideways power—the predominant form of power expression outside the formal boss–subordinate relationship—is absolutely essential if managers are to get their jobs done. Downward power—getting work done through subordinates—represents a much smaller portion of a manager's time and effort than heretofore considered. The bulk of a manager's efforts is often spent outside the work unit, dealing with other department heads, divisions, or subsidiaries, over whom he or she has no formal control.

Developing, using, and maintaining multiple sources of power other than formal position becomes essential for today's managers in complex organizations. When managers move outside clear-cut authority relationships to get things done, dependence on others is greater than the formal power and control given to people to do these jobs. According to Kotter (1979), "Power dynamics, under these circumstances, are inevitable and are needed to make organizations function well."

Models of Organization

How we view power directions is often a function of the conceptual model that we use to understand behavior in organizations. All of us utilize our mental maps to determine how organizations actually and ideally should function. Sometimes we use these models as tools for diagnosis and other times we use them as idealized versions of how life should be in organizations. It is not unusual for us to confuse our idealized model with how organizations actually do function.

Our concern in this book is with deciding on a model that comes closer to representing organizational reality, even if it departs from our idealized models. It is this reality that OD consultants have to work with before they attempt to move an organization to some other "reality." Two authors have prepared several models. Baldridge (1971) describes three organizational archetypes—bureaucratic, collegial, and political. Pfeffer (1981) suggests four organizational decision models—rational, bureaucratic, organized anarchy, and political. Distilling from these various alternatives, we present three organizational models of our own and relate them to the power directions discussed in the previous section. As we shall see, our three models treat power directions differently, and thereby affect which types of power we attend to, ignore, or, possibly, try to eliminate.

Rational/Bureaucratic Model

The Rational/Bureaucratic model is most likely to be espoused by traditional management scholars, and one that most of us know well. It emphasizes rationally structured systems, built on division of labor and job specialization in a functional structure. Authority is top down, and utilizes formal communication channels, usually vertical, and well-defined policies and procedures. Organizational goals are clearly specified to direct efforts of employees toward greater efficiency. Formal systems and policies are used to provide control, predictability, and stability.

If we as OD practitioners use or even prefer this model, how are we likely to view power in organizations? First, power is seen as hierarchical and so gaining formal approval from top management becomes the sine qua non of successful organizational change. The focus of change is directed toward improving the way superiors use power to manage subordinates. Managerial effectiveness is equated with subordinate performance, and it is achieved through what is known as humanistic management. The leader acts with greater sensitivity to soften the impact of downward power. Although the humanistic leadership labels have changed over the years, Theory Y Management, the Considerate Leader, and the Situational Leader are all concepts that are conditioned by a concern with the exercise and effects of downward power.

Upward power in the Rational/Bureaucratic model is generally seen as disruptive and non-legitimate. Under limited circumstances, it may be tolerated or even encouraged if its expression is narrowly controlled, such as in the use of Management by Objectives or Quality Circles. Sideways power receives virtually no consideration in this model, since vertical authority is the prescribed decision-making channel; integration occurs only at the apex of the pyramid.

Collegial/Consensus Model

The Collegial/Consensus model places emphasis on interpersonal and small group behavior in organizations (Argyris, 1962). Rules, policies, and procedures are relaxed, or even disbanded, in order to enhance interaction and participation in decision making. In contrast to the Rational/Bureaucratic model, formal authority relationships are minimized in the Collegial/Consensus model. The need for direction and control is replaced by teamwork in the spirit of "all for one, one for all." Individual contributions are highly valued, within a focus on collaboration and integration.

The view here is that human involvement and participation are good for both the organization and the individual. Equalizing the distribution of authority is assumed to lead to better decision making and fuller commitment to decisions.

Upward power is seen as legitimate and encouraged in this model. All forms of power redistribution are part of the organizational "should's," such as an Employee Bill of Rights, profit-sharing, worker councils, and employee representation on the board of directors. A flat organizational structure, appropriate to a professional group, reflects the high priority given to upward power.

In the Collegial/Consensus model, downward power is barely tolerated, and then only in limited situations in which peer pressure proves ineffective, such as in firing a troublesome employee. Sideways power proves unnecessary because concensus and collaboration are the accepted norms.

Pluralistic/Political Model

The Pluralistic/Political Model sees organizations as composed of differing interest groups. Each party pursues its own goals, sometimes on selfish grounds but often for well-intended reasons based on its view of what is best for the organization as a whole. Conflict is viewed as inevitable and a normal part of the way things get done. Political behavior results when an attempt at influence is countered by another interested party or group.

According to Cyert and March (1964) (among the first to espouse a political theory of organizations), the objectives of the firm are arrived at through a process of bargaining among and between coalitions as they respond to environmental changes. Basic to the idea of a coalition is the expectation that those with similar interests will band together to influence the direction of the organization toward goals attributed to it by the coalition. Power becomes the intervening variable between desired outcomes and actual results.

Kotter (1977, 1985) sees power and political behavior arising naturally out of the inherent interdependency in most managerial jobs. Power and political behavior are dependent on a wide range of people outside the formal authority chain to get decisions made and work accomplished—for example, in dealing with suppliers, government officials, bankers, and technical experts. Lacking formal authority over these people, the use of power and influence becomes essential for effective managerial functioning.

The Pluralistic/Political Model allows for all forms of power expression. Power is truly everywhere and naturally used by those desiring to fulfill their work-related objectives. The arena of work activity expands beyond the traditional superior–subordinate relationship to include the entire organization. For example, a product manager in the marketing department may discover that one plant in manufacturing is producing defective products. The product manager may go directly to the VP of manufacturing (sideways and upwards power) and convince him to fix things. This VP will then have to influence his subordinates to correct the problems (downward power). The product manager may even have to involve his boss (upward power) to bring about the change.

Sideways power is recognized as a necessary and frequently exercised component of managerial effectiveness. Groups across the organization must compete for scarce resources, and they are horizontally dependent on one another to perform their jobs on schedule. Similarly, upward power takes on importance as individuals lower on the organization chart attempt to exercise influence over senior managers with greater control over needed resources.

Downward power is important, too, to assure that the needs of the overall organization, as perceived by the powerholders at the top, are being considered in decision making at lower levels. Sometimes downward power is required to force a solution on conflicting parties. However, downward power can lose its potency when lower level units also possess significant power, such as found in conflicts with a labor union or with a group of prima donna research scientists.

Organizational Realities

Which of the three models, or archetypes, comes closer to matching organizational reality? We agree with Cyert and March (1964), Baldridge (1971), and Pfeffer (1981), among other organizational theorists, who advance the Pluralistic/Political Model as a more accurate representation of how organizations and managers really function. It is not because people in organizations are greedy or corrupt, but simply because people are different and resources are scattered and limited. A compromise must be reached if the organization is to continue to function.

Moreover, Kotter (1985, 1986) contends that today's organizations possess even greater diversity and interdependence than companies of a few years ago. Technologies have proliferated, economic resources have become constrained, and competition has intensified. Unfortunately, according to Kotter, "The recentness of these changes is one of the key reasons why many people are only partially aware of the realities" of the Pluralistic/Political model.

The Pluralistic/Political model is, in our opinion, a less idealized model than the other two models. These other models may be worth striving for in certain situations, because research evidence suggests that the Rational/Bureaucratic model may be more effective in dealing with simple technologies and stable environments, while the Collegial/Consensus model fits better with more complex and uncertain environments (Lawrence and Lorsch, 1967).

However, these two "desirable" models for unique situations often work out differently in practice (Greiner and Schein,

1981; Schein and Greiner, 1977). The Rational/Bureaucratic model can produce overly restrictive formal systems that stifle initiative and reduce responsiveness to change. And the Collegial/ Consensus model can create anarchic behavior at lower levels that undermines teamwork and, ultimately, the firm. We also know from research on human personality that not all people want to work in teams; some people prefer greater structure (Lorsch and Morse, 1974). The point is that both models, even in their most perfect states, will always contain strong threads of the Pluralistic/Political perspective.

Therefore, the key to understanding power in organizations is to acknowledge the pervasive reality of political behavior across and throughout all organizational forms. It means accepting power as natural and necessary to decision making regardless of formal structure. By using a Pluralistic/Political model, we can diagnose the many and varied expressions of power in a broader and more unbiased way. Adhering to either the Rational/Bureaucratic or Collegial/Consensus models may blind us to many aspects of power-oriented behavior.

Managing Those You Do Not Manage

To explore further and illustrate the Pluralistic/Political model, we conclude this chapter with a more comprehensive account of sideways power. These horizontal situations involve people trying to influence other people over whom they have little formal control. Today's organizations, with interrelated technologies and requirements for rapid response to complex problems, all require considerable use of sideways power. Gaining approval, competing for scarce resources, and obtaining cooperation require managers to develop bases of power beyond positional authority.

Leonard Sayles, in *Managerial Behavior* (1964), delineates several types of external relationships. Based upon his research as well as our own field studies, three such types are: Service, Competitive, and Work Flow relationships. The following case examples illustrate their sideways power dynamics.

The Service Relationship

In the service relationship, the manager usually has a staff or advisory role. He or she must gain approval from others, outside formal authority channels, to implement a staff project. Success in such positions requires more than technical expertise. The most brilliant of legal, financial, or personnel reports are worthless unless they can be put into action by other people, who must be convinced to accept another's recommendations.

Jack, a financial director in a medium sized chemical company, provides a good account of his activities over three years to win acceptance. "It hasn't been easy," he says, "because the finance department is still considered a 'necessary evil' by most other departments." In Jack's company, marketing has greater departmental power than production, research, or finance.

Jack always begins his projects by talking first with the marketing department. He purposely selects projects that meet a well-defined need from marketing's point of view. He then presells a program by discussing it with informal leaders in marketing, who are friends of his. In doing so, he exposes a need and then announces he can meet it. Jack uses selective information, highlighting the positive aspects of a program. His expertise, control over information, and alliances with others are the power bases for many of these influence strategies. Convincing others in the company to go along with his ideas and those of his staff is time-consuming, but a major part of his job. Jack feels his success in these endeavors and the improving performance and credibility of his department are worth the additional effort at political influence.

The Competitive Relationship

In a competitive relationship, the manager must compete with other peer level managers for organizational resources, such as money and personnel. Failure to be successful in the competitive relationship can have a negative impact on the ability of a manager to motivate his or her people.

Mary, manager of information services, posed to us a serious problem she was facing; she had neglected to build her own power in negotiating salary increases for her staff. Mary had done an excellent job all year in motivating her staff to operate at maximum efficiency and effectiveness. However, she was unsuccessful in an important competitive relationship, the annual personnel evaluation in her division. Mary's group received fewer promotional slots and merit increases than any other group.

Mary's staff had all done outstanding jobs and expected to be rewarded accordingly. However, Mary had to announce that there would be only one promotion and merit increases would be smaller. Later, her staff members became aware of the larger number of promotions and monetary rewards accorded to people in other groups. Motivation dropped in Mary's group, and one member requested a transfer.

Reflecting, Mary said, "I thought it would be obvious to everyone that my people had done a good job. What I didn't realize was that, ahead of time, I hadn't convinced the other supervisors at my level of that fact, and some of them had more influence with our division head. So I lost."

The Work Flow Relationship

In certain businesses, the final product is dependent upon the work of many units operating in sequence; there is a preset way in which the work moves from one unit to another. Increased efficiencies in one unit will not be apparent if the next unit does not agree to speed up as well. The manager of one unit must therefore negotiate with managers of other units to get a job done the way he or she feels it should be done.

One situation, that of a superintendent in a large steel company, provides a good example of how one operates in a work flow relationship. According to the superintendent, the railroad that delivers slabs to his heating furnaces for heating prior to rolling has its own way of doing things. Even though the superintendent places orders as he needs them, the railroad waits until it has a container load before delivering any. In order to keep his lines running and meet customer delivery dates, the superintendent, however, needs the slabs as soon as possible.

The superintendent described how he changed this situation. "I already had a friendship with the railroad supervisor, so I invited him to lunch. Then I suggested an exchange of favors. The railroad supervisor knows I can be of help to him in the future. He knows that one day he may be on the other side of the table."

The superintendent used quid pro quo to change the work situation. He now gets regular, smaller deliveries so he can do the job the way he feels it should be done.

Implications for OD

Warren Bennis, in his book, *Organization Development* (1969), predicts what can happen to OD if it does not acknowledge the reality of the Pluralistic/Political model. "The organization development consultant tends to use the truth–love model when it may not be appropriate and has no alternative model to guide his practice under conditions of distrust . . . and conflict. . . . This means that in pluralistic power situations . . . organization development may not reach its desired goal. . . . This may explain why OD has been reasonably successful where power is relatively centralized . . . organization development has not met with success in diffuse power structures."

Understanding the realities of power with one's blinders off is essential for the healthy survival of the OD field. We have listed three directional expressions of power and their relationship to three models in use so that we can reexamine our own ways of diagnosing organizations, as well as question our own attitudes toward various expressions of power in them.

Few would deny that OD's model in use has for many years been dominated by the Collegial/Consensus model. OD has focused mainly on upward power within formal work groups, thereby ignoring or denying other expressions of power. If OD categorizes other forms of power as neurotic, selfish, or even unnecessary, it fails to recognize that work-related power is expressed naturally in a variety of ways across the entire work environment. The Pluralistic/Political model, in contrast, assumes that the expression of power is essential in reaching a trade-off between vested interests and organizational goals.

For OD to let go of the Collegial/Consensus model as a primary model for understanding and influencing behavior in organizations does not mean abandoning OD's traditional values of trust, openness, and collaboration or its techniques of team building and interpersonal feedback. Instead, these values and techniques must be treated as limited expressions of power to be supplemented by many other forms of influence that are selectively applied in a particular political context.

3

Developing Power Bases

Power bases are composed of unique resources over which a manager has control. These bases determine a manager's available power strategies for influencing others. You cannot pay someone more money if you do not have a power base that controls financial resources. Without power bases, you can do little to influence someone else. Or with limited bases, you have only a narrow selection of power strategies available. Hence, power bases are pivotal in the power equation.

Beyond Position Power

A formal position in the organization is the most widely defined base of power. Building on Weber's original sociological theory of bureaucracy, French and Raven (1959) refer to position power for the psychological "legitimacy" it lends to a manager's influence attempts, while Schein (1980) describes it in terms of its "rational–legal" implications.

Position power is basically a combination of one's job title, job description, and prescribed responsibilities. It provides the incumbent with the formal authority needed to control and direct the activities of one's subordinates. The tasks of selecting, evaluating, rewarding, and even terminating subordinates are essential ingredients of position power. It also includes the dispensing (or withholding) of resources, such as merit increases, promotional opportunities, coveted job assignments, and vacation time. Position power can encompass the reward and coercion power bases referred to by French and Raven.

Although position power appears to be a strong base of power, the inexperienced manager with a seemingly prestigious title can be deluded into thinking she has more power in the organization than she actually does. In today's complex organizations, where the Pluralistic/Political model is a reality, all forms of power expression—upward, downward, and sideways—are necessary to get the job done. Position power, therefore, is of limited value except in the case of downward influence when it is contained in the relationship between superior and subordinate. Position power proves of little use when trading or negotiating with others of equal or higher levels in the organization or with lower level managers remote from one's department. For others in the organization, and outside it, job titles become a reference point for what you do rather than how much clout you have.

For example, we observed a new and ambitious vice president of corporate purchasing who assumed that, because of his position power, those managers at lower levels in departments outside purchasing (plant purchasing managers) would readily accept his influence. After a few of his written directives were ignored and suggestions at meetings were dismissed, the limitations of position power became clear. At this point, the manager began to develop additional bases of power.

In going beyond position power, we shall discuss two broad kinds of power bases—individual and departmental. Individual bases relate to particular abilities and background experiences rather than to the job itself. These individual bases are transportable and remain with the manager as he or she moves from situation to situation. Departmental power bases, however, are grounded in the work unit itself rather than in the skills and abilities of the individual. The weak head of a strong and powerful department has a great deal of influence over others only as long as he or she stays in that particular position.

Both individual and departmental power bases are dynamic. Unlike position power, these other power bases can be developed and expanded. So, too, they can be eroded by others who seek to expand their own bases of power. By developing both individual and departmental bases, a manager can use them separately or in combination to achieve his or her objectives. Not only is more and diverse power better, but these multiple bases of power can provide an even stronger repertoire of power strategies from which to influence others.

Individual Power Bases

We have categorized eight potential bases of individual power under three broad types: *Knowledge, Personality,* and *Others' Support.*

Knowledge
 expert
 information
 tradition
Personality
 charisma
 reputation
 professional credibility
Others' Support
 political access
 staff support

These various bases are drawn partly from earlier psychological and sociological theories, such as Weber's charisma and French and Raven's referent power in the *personality* category, as well as from Raven (1965), Pettigrew (1975), and our own field observations. Exercising influence in today's Pluralistic/Political organizations requires a wide range of power bases, as it encompasses all boundaries of power expression—upward, downward, and sideways.

Knowledge

With modern organizations increasingly populated with "knowledge workers," this broad category of power should receive the attention of all managers, including OD consultants. It is composed of the power bases expertise, information, and tradition.

Expert power refers to the possession of a specific body of knowledge acquired either through formal academic training or job experience. One is able to influence others because one is perceived to know more about a particular subject than anyone else. Lawyers and accountants, for example, exercise substantial influence over those who do not possess similar expertise.

Expertise can be especially valuable to individuals new to organizations. The M.B.A. degree, for example, provides the entrant with at least a starting base of power to achieve work-related objectives. In several organizations we know, the Harvard M.B.A. creates an aura of anticipation, intimidation, or sometimes skepticism from employees. Whatever the reaction, all ears and eyes are on that person. Expertise is also useful to those blocked from gaining other sources of power. It is hardly coincidental that women and minorities initially gained access to organizations via staff jobs (expertise) rather than through line positions.

Misuse of expertise, however, can render it worthless. When the expert overuses technical jargon, others not accustomed to the lexicon will become alienated. Attempts to exercise *expert* power beyond one's area of expertise tends to reduce the value placed on that expertise.

Information power allows one to influence others by creating information, withholding it, distorting it, or redirecting the flow toward selected recipients.

If you attempt to influence others at a meeting, you are more likely to do so if you have more relevant information than anyone else. If you are in a central channel for receiving important information, you may be able to get what you want by redirecting the flow of data to determine who sees what, when, and in what order.

One vice president of human resources is well known in

his firm for his information base of power. When we first met him, one thing was clear—he was never in his office. Rather, he could usually be found perched on the side of someone's desk, "chatting." Many dubbed him "the roving vice president." But he was not roving for fun. He was acquiring information that he later used as a resource to influence others.

Another manager in an aerospace firm uses the network of one of her subordinates, a staff analyst, to gain control over information. The analyst has a friend in computer operations, and he is able to find out what projects in the rest of the organization may not make their deadlines, which ones are of high priority, and what projects are to be cancelled. He passes this information on to his boss who is always well prepared for project review meetings.

A third type of knowledge power is *tradition*. By virtue of seniority in an organization, an individual can acquire historical knowledge about the company and use it as a base from which to influence others. Long-term experience in a company allows one to evoke stories and myths as a way of controlling the behavior of newer employees. Myths can neither be proven nor disproven. Without evidence to the contrary, it may be unwise to go against the behavior suggested as appropriate by the myth.

One young manager described to us how he went to his boss, a senior vice president, with an innovative proposal. She read the proposal, nodded, and then said, "Interesting idea. But are you aware that we considered a similar proposal six years ago and the CEO rejected it . . . he's very conservative." This statement stopped the young manager in his tracks. Who was he to question the CEO? And the senior vice president had been there for twenty-five years. "Surely she must know what she is talking about," he said to himself, "or does she?"

Tradition, then, becomes a strong power base from which to employ a defensive strategy to resist change. The young manager either accepts the story as true and does nothing further about his proposal, or he takes a big risk by going above the senior vice president to her boss. In either case, the burden of the decision and its outcome are put squarely on the shoulders of the subordinate.

Personality

Personality is a rich source of power; included in it are the aspects of charisma, reputation, and professional credibility. *Charisma* is defined as the ability to inspire devotion and enthusiasm from others. The power of a magnetic personality, such as Lawrence of Arabia, Joan of Arc, Martin Luther King, or John F. Kennedy, is most commonly found in leader–follower situations involving mass politics or emotional causes. However, business leaders, such as Lee Iaccoca of Chrysler and Jack Welch of GE, are also charismatic leaders who attract other capable leaders and spark greater commitment from the work force.

The manager with charisma maneuvers easily around the formal system. He or she can reach informally across hierarchical levels to find the best person for the job, work around roadblocks, and inspire others to follow his or her lead. The charismatic leader has strong persuasive skills, allowing him or her many successes based on the force of personality alone.

Unfortunately, not too many of us are gifted with charisma, although there is the possibility that managers can be trained to be more outgoing and evocative in their emotional appeals.

Reputation is a base of power stemming from others who have a favorable opinion of your work and capabilities. Terms such as *thought leader, golden boy,* or *winner,* refer to people with a power base of reputation. It is rarely based on one specific accomplishment; rather, it stems from continuous reports of good work and other such favorable accomplishments.

Plans of action recommended by a manager with reputation are usually listened to attentively by others, if not accepted at face value. That person is perceived as a winner, and his coattails look inviting. Recommendations by the person with a good reputation are less likely to be carefully scrutinized; the person is usually assumed to be correct.

Senior level people new to an organization usually have a beginning power base based on reputation. The organization is rife with rumors about the person's prior accomplishments in her former company. It is widely known how much time and money went into the recruitment effort and how lucky the company is to get her.

Nonetheless, there are always people waiting in the wings to discredit a positive image. Even without mistakes, the halo effect eventually wears off when someone else emerges as the new golden girl.

A third power base linked to personality is *professional credibility.* Participation in industry meetings and professional associations through speeches and articles not only increases your exposure and reputation among others outside your company but strengthens your own power base back home. With such a base, your dependency on the organization is lessened. You can allow yourself greater freedom of expression and take more risks. If your efforts fail, outside credibility provides you with career mobility.

One marketing manager we know had very little success within his own company because his boss continually blocked his ideas. To counteract that, he began writing articles for a leading trade publication. A senior manager read one of the articles and promptly promoted the marketing manager to a position as his assistant.

Others' Support

In keeping with the old adage of "It's who you know that counts," the support of others, both external and internal to one's work unit, is often an essential power base. *Political access* refers to the ability to call upon networks of relationships within the organization. With such access, a manager can deal directly with a key decision maker or find out what is really happening. By picking up the telephone and getting an immediate reading on a situation, a manager can alter his work priorities to accommodate the yet to be announced crisis.

Political access is a base that is usually developed informally. Company sports programs, incompany management training sessions, and luncheons provide opportunities to meet individuals with whom one does not usually work. This base is cultivated over the years, and later becomes the Old Boy's/Girl's Network. The superintendent in the steel company, described in

Chapter 2, had political access. He was able to go directly to the railroad supervisor and convince him to change the pace of slab deliveries.

In another company, a manager of personnel has political access to a senior vice president. They met originally at a company orientation program, and subsequently the latter executive rose rapidly in the company. Today the manager of personnel makes a point of sitting next to his old friend on the daily commuter train. The importance of these rides is evident when the manager enters the office to announce: "Put more people on the transportation project; we are relocating a division to Florida." "Be prepared; there is going to be a major personnel change in the foods division." "Don't put too much effort into the appraisal program for Services people; it will probably be cancelled." Formal memos describing these events usually arrive one or two weeks later. The manager's work group is always prepared, thanks to political access.

By developing *staff support* as a power base, a manager can multiply the amount of resources and influence strategies available to him. The astute manager can rely on subordinates to develop and use their own political access, provide information, and bring untapped expertise to a situation. Moreover, subordinates can serve as a sounding board, especially when influence attempts are unsuccessful and a new game plan must be devised.

You develop and maintain staff support by realizing and accepting where your power bases end and theirs begin. It is necessary to be open and honest with subordinates, informing them about the strategies you are pursuing, and asking for their involvement and support. At the same time, beware of undermining their power bases by claiming undue credit for yourself. Activities such as luncheons, meetings, and extensive telephone calls, all in the cause of implementing one of your staff group's ideas, need to be explained to the staff. Otherwise, staff members can feel they are doing all the real work while the boss is usurping the limelight. By keeping staff members fully apprised of the work-related reasons for your activities and involving them in their implementation, you can increase the pool of your power resources and, at the same time, maintain the power bases of your subordinates.

Departmental Power Bases

Departmental power bases are directly related to what the work unit does. As would be predicted by a Pluralistic/Political model, the power of different departments varies among organizations (Perrow, 1970); in some companies, sales is the most powerful department, while in others it is finance or research and development. And departmental power can change over time, depending on economic conditions, technological breakthroughs, and government legislation.

Departmental power bases are therefore as dynamic as individual power bases and also need to be developed, used, and maintained, or else they can be eroded by other department heads seeking to expand the power of their own units.

Formal notions of departmental power suggest that it varies according to objective factors, such as the number of employees or assets being controlled. However, the correlation between these physical factors and actual power can be quite low. A more meaningful way to view departmental power is to consider the contribution of the department to the functioning of the total organization. Based upon the work of Hickson and associates (1971), there are three underlying dimensions that determine departmental power bases: ability to cope with uncertainty facing the total organization; low substitutability or not being easily replaced; and centrality in the work flow of the company.

Ability to Cope with Uncertainty

Organizational environments are always uncertain, so departments that can cope effectively with uncertainty can increase their power within the organization. One approach is simply to minimize uncertainty. For example, survival is the most pressing concern of any new company, and there is great concern about whether or not that company's product is salable. Thus, if the sales department is able to secure firm future orders, it becomes the most powerful department.

Providing information that *reduces* uncertainty is a second way a department can increase its power base. If the organization needs better knowledge about future trends in order to plan in the present, departments that provide such information, such as economic forecasting or market research, rise in power.

A third strategy is to *absorb* uncertainty. The rise in power of personnel departments in some U.S. companies can be attributed to their ability to absorb uncertainty regarding equal employment opportunity. In the late 1960s and early 1970s, there was a great deal of fear regarding affirmative action efforts; the cost of overcoming discrimination and complying with government regulations was escalating; class action discrimination suits ran into the millions of dollars. The more powerful personnel departments were those who rushed to the aid of their companies and developed ways to cope with this uncertainty. They trained people in how to reduce discrimination in selection and promotion, developed corrective policies, and dealt directly with the government during compliance reviews. As a result, their staffs and budgets were increased.

Substitutability

A department can be said to have a power base of low substitutability if no other department in the organization can perform its work functions or activities. The rise and fall of data processing units illustrates this elusive power base. Fifteen years ago, computer services held a great deal of power in many companies. Few people could understand its activities, much less the technical vocabulary of its members. The head of computer services could dictate lead times and turnaround times for all projects. Other managers had very little say because they were dependent on that unit for information output.

Today, the power of data processing groups has markedly declined because they have lost their power base of low substitutability. With the advent of the microcomputer, managers now can input and analyze their own data. Most of us are conversant with modems, microchips, and software packages. The days of an elite group knowing "computer speak" are over.

Centrality

A work unit holds a power base of centrality if other departments are very dependent on it in the work flow. A claims department in an insurance company has centrality. If it stops producing, large numbers of other units whose work follows from this group cannot function. In a high tech company, the research and development department must create new products because company survival is at stake. Errors made by the scheduling group in a Big Eight accounting firm can temporarily immobilize the firm by not assigning the right people to an audit engagement.

Dynamics of Departmental Power

Departmental power bases are not totally within any one department's control. Environmental changes can add to or diminish a department's power. If there is a downturn in the economy, sudden pressure can be placed on sales to reduce this uncertainty. If the economy improves, power may shift to research and development for developing new products. In the same company, during tense labor negotiations, the power of the industrial relations department increases. Nevertheless, much discretion remains for departments to increase their power, and politically astute department heads become skillful at doing so.

Coping with Uncertainty

By being sensitive to environmental demands and areas of vulnerability to the company, a department can increase its power. The key here is to be alert to the company's real needs and to absorb or minimize that uncertainty. The response of some personnel departments to affirmative action pressures demonstrates the efficacy of this approach. The financial director, Jack, described in Chapter 2, increased his department's power by selecting projects that met a well-defined need, then announcing he could meet that need.

Another and more complex way departments cope with uncertainty is to create uncertainty themselves and then step forward to be recognized as the only group able to resolve it. Creating uncertainty in organizations by reorganization has been occurring since ancient times:

It seemed that every time we were beginning to form up in teams we would be reorganized. I was to learn later in life that we tend to meet any new situation by reorganizing; and what a wonderful method it can be for creating an illusion of progress while producing confusion, inefficiency, and demoralization. (Petronius Arbiter, 200 B.C.)

During any reorganization, confusion and uncertainty reign. The department or group that masterminds the change is often perceived to be the only one who can cope with it. Hence, power accrues for that department. We have seen this happen when a task force is appointed to oversee a major organizational change. Phones start ringing as people try to establish who is on the task force, and rumors spread about what it may do.

Developing Substitutability

Substitutability can be acquired and maintained by departments through shielding from others how their work is actually performed. Crozier, in *The Bureaucratic Phenomenon* (1963), describes how workers in the maintenance department in an automated cigar factory created this protective mystique. They never discussed with machine operators or engineers how the equipment was maintained. Moreover, they removed any information from the files that might make their work more predictable. Whenever anything went wrong, there was no substitute for the maintenance department.

Senior managers concerned with efficiency often try to reduce the substitutability of other departments below them. Formal systems and procedures are used to routinize the work flow and eliminate the number of people who can perform certain tasks. These efforts are countered by managers trying to maintain their power base of low substitutability, who argue that their functions are too complex or dynamic to be routinized.

Increasing Centrality

If a department already has centrality or is about to receive greater importance because of a reorganization, it is an opportune position to be in for acquiring additional resources. Attention is focused on that department because with it, goes the future of the company.

In the case of Mega Corporation described in Chapter 8, the new head of marketing lobbied for and received permission to recruit all the new college graduates with high potential from a local university. His rationale was that marketing was deemed by the new corporate strategy to be a department of high priority and that he was personally well connected at the university. As a result, the human resources department lost responsibility for recruiting future managers.

Implications for OD

An OD consultant must understand his or her own power bases as well as the power bases of those he or she attempts to influence in the organization. Without such awareness, the OD consultant acts with a severe handicap.

Is the line manager resistant to your restructuring plan because it will have a negative impact on the informal flow of communication, thereby reducing her information power base? To what extent would a new goal-setting program be viewed by the budgeting manager as reducing his department's base of substitutability? "Why are there so many meetings around here? Perhaps we need to reduce meeting times," thinks the OD consultant. He is unaware that such meetings also provide arenas for the development and use of expertise, information, and reputation bases of power.

In many organizations with which we are familiar, OD operates from a low positional base of power. Therefore, it is essential for the OD consultant to turn to knowledge, personality, and others' support for establishing a stronger power base. Seminars can be used for increasing expertise, and the application of techniques such as action research develops an information base. Those consultants with charisma can volunteer to act as lead persons on projects; after a few successes, their power base of reputation grows. Staff support within the human resources department is essential so that outside executives will not pit traditional personnel activities against revolutionary OD. To the extent OD is viewed as a threat, tradition may be frequently encountered as a defensive base of power; here OD needs to avoid attacking directly any of the "sacred cows" of the organization's culture.

Many OD consultants or groups with lower levels of power fail to develop political access. Not recognizing the political nature of organizations, some OD groups remain isolated in corporate headquarters. They fail to court line managers in the operating groups who make the major decisions. Decentralizing OD to work directly for line managers can make it more relevant and powerful.

OD has often missed opportunities to demonstrate its ability to cope with uncertainty by not immersing itself in issues of major concern to the growth and survival of the business. Power is lost when OD focuses only on team building in minor departments lacking centrality. On the other hand, strategic planning, a vital area in which OD has long been absent, is a rich opportunity for making a contribution, as will be shown later in the Mega Case.

4

Using Power Strategies

Asking the reader to consider power strategies may conjure up images of Machiavellian pursuits, military tactics, and even the witches of *Macbeth* stirring up "toil and trouble." Several popular myths hold that power strategies are innate in certain personalities with a strong need for power, that such strategies are rarely preplanned, and that those who consciously strategize will not admit it. However, as we shall see in this chapter, a vast majority of managers can and do purposely use power strategies, and they are quite willing to discuss it.

The most active power strategies are day-to-day attempts to influence people over whom we do not have formal control. When we lack direct authority, yet need approval of resources from others, power strategies must be employed. Even for managers to influence their subordinates in today's organizations, they need power strategies beyond position because subordinates may have strong power bases of their own. These noncompliant subordinates can seek to control their own career destinies by forming sideways coalitions and using social networks to go above the boss.

A major portion of this chapter is based on a power strategies research study conducted by Virginia Schein and her associates (1987). Over three hundred managers in the United States and United Kingdom participated in an interview and questionnaire examination of power strategies that managers actually use to achieve work-related objectives. We will report the results of this research through the voices of different managers who describe their various power strategies as well as through supporting quantitative data from the questionnaire responses.

Managerial Voices

Corporate Planner

Ned is a corporate planner in a large electronics products company. He joined the company six years ago, following receipt of his M.B.A. from a leading business school. Last year he successfully introduced the concept of market segmentation into a major corporate division. Ned explained to us how he did it.

> Since the day I entered this company I have tried to maintain an image of a winner. I had many good job offers and the company's efforts to lure me here were active and well known. I tried to keep the "hotshot" image going as long as possible. For one thing, I went around the company offering expert assistance to people. These favors helped to play up my positive image.
>
> When I was ready to implement market segmentation, I went back to many of these same people. As I heard later, they felt, "He must know what he is talking about. I better get on his bandwagon, even if I don't understand it."
>
> In seeking acceptance for my plan, I would get information from others and then use only their positive comments in discussing ideas with others. When I would hear of problems, I would often blame them on our past failure to do market segmentation. Finally, I developd a good rapport with the CEO and two of his key executives. I was able to cut across lines of authority and go directly to them to present my plan.

Publications Coordinator

Jane is the publications coordinator for a large university where she has been for five years after previous experience in a publishing firm. A year ago the university decided to hire an outside design team to produce all of its publications, and a university committee was selected to recommend a design team to the vice dean, who had the final say. It was very important to Jane that her first choice be selected, and she explained to us how she accomplished that objective.

> First of all, I made sure I was involved in the selection of the committee members. I put as many of my allies — those who would go along with my ideas — on the committee as I could. I prescreened all the design teams. This gave me more information about the teams than any of the other committee members had. I made a point of finding out what criteria for selection were important to most of the committee members. In discussing the team of my choice, I made sure to highlight these factors.
>
> Finally, I delayed the committee process. As the deadline got closer, the vice dean became anxious that a decision be made by the committee. Everyone recognized that I had more background and information in these matters. The committee members, especially the vice dean, were quite willing to listen to my opinions.

What do these two managerial voices tell us? We can see that managers do indeed use power strategies to accomplish their objectives, and they can clearly articulate them. Both Ned and Jane had set certain strategies in motion by establishing a positive image and locating allies long before a definite need was established. They then used a range of strategies emanating from specific power bases. Ned relied on a combination of expertise, information, reputation, and political access to cut around hierarchy and convince the CEO of his plan. Jane used expertise, information, staff support, and professional credibility to delay the committee and increase dependence on her for a decision.

Interview Study

These two voices, as well as those of the superintendent in the steel company and the financial director in the chemical company in Chapter 3, were taken from an interview study conducted by Virginia Schein and her associates. They interviewed managers and executives from a broad array of organizations about their various power strategies. The total group of interviewees consisted of eight lower level, twenty-six middle level and forty senior level managers. Sixty were men and fourteen women. Most of these managers were in their early forties and had spent about twelve years at their present companies. The range of industries included manufacturing, service, and nonprofit institutions.

In the interviews, managers were asked to describe a work situation not involving their subordinates in which they were successful in achieving their objectives. Then they were asked what strategies and tactics they used and what power bases or resources they used. These same questions were asked again about an unsuccessful situation.

One of the surprising outcomes was the ease with which these managers discussed their power strategies. Many of them stated at the outset, "It's about time someone asked me what I *really* do in getting things done around here." The situations described by them dealt with meeting specific objectives such as getting a new policy approved, implementing a new program, gaining support for a new subsidiary, and selling staff services to line operations. Most of their influence attempts were focused on either peer level managers, such as other department heads, project leaders, and regional officers; or on senior level decision makers, such as board members, CEOs, and executive committees.

The first goal of the study was to define what power strategies were actually used by these managers. The seventy-four interviews generated 148 situations, which were divided in half and read by two research assistants. Each assistant read the interviews, and together they extracted 175 statements of specific power strategies used. Each reader then took the others' statements and sorted them into eighteen broad categories. Three doctoral candidates also independently sorted the strategy statements again within the eighteen categories. The average rate of agreement among these three reviewers was 70 percent.

Table 4-1 lists the final eighteen categories of influence strategies in order of frequency of use. The most frequently used strategy was develop alliances and coalitions. Here managers stated they "established a coalition," "gained support of peers," "formed allies among peers," and "developed rapport with groups capable of bringing about change." In second place was present a persuasive viewpoint where managers said they "logically presented ideas," "emphasized the innovative aspects of ideas," "persuaded others," and "used a formal presentation." Other top influence strategies were: deal directly with key decision makers; use data to convince others; focus on needs of target group; and work around roadblocks. Table 4-2 illustrates specific approaches used within each of these broad categories.

By then using a questionnaire, Schein sought to determine

Table 4-1

Types of Strategies in Use

Form alliances and coalitions
Present a persuasive viewpoint
Deal directly with key decision makers
Use data to convince others
Focus on needs of the target group
Work around roadblocks
Exaggerate information
Use personal attributes
Use contacts for information
Surround self with competent others
Deal with others socially
Be persistent
Offer favors/monetary rewards
Use threats
Commit the uncommitted
Use organizational rules
Give guarantees
Discredit the opposition

Table 4–2
Specific Strategies in Use

Deal Directly with Key Decision Makers
- Identify influential individuals and direct proposals toward them
- Gain access to key decision makers
- Have formal review meeting with senior management
- Presell idea to key decision maker
- Arrange meetings with influential decision makers

Use Data to Convince Others
- Collect data supporting idea
- Obtain great amount of data
- Rely on empirical observations
- Demonstrate estimated savings

Focus on Needs of Target Group
- Research client's needs
- Give personal service to each client
- Write proposal in terms of target group
- Meet the needs of the decision makers

Work Around Roadblocks
- Obtain assistance of key decision maker's peer
- Work around the boss
- Negotiate a settlement

if these same eighteen power strategies are used across different cultures, and if the quantitative data support the findings from the subjective interview methodology. Schein also sought to learn more about which strategies were associated with successful and unsuccessful outcomes.

The eighteen influence strategies formed the basis of the questionnaire, which was administered to 251, 194 men and 57 women, managers in the United States and United Kingdom. Sixteen percent of the managers were in lower level positions; 48 percent in middle level jobs; and 36 percent in senior management positions. Most managers were in their mid-thirties and had been with their present companies about six to seven years.

The questionnaire instructed each manager to: "Consider a past situation not involving your subordinates in which you were successful in accomplishing your objectives." The eighteen influence categories were listed, and the respondent was asked to place a check next to the strategies used in that situation. On another page, the same list of strategies and instructions was presented, except here the manager was asked to consider an unsuccessful situation.

As shown in Table 4–3, there is a remarkable similarity in the frequency of strategies used, both between the questionnaire

Table 4–3

Comparison of Strategies in Use

	Managers		
	U.S.	U.K	U.S.
	(Questionnaire)		(Interview)
Specific Strategy	N = 180	N = 71	N = 74
Present persuasive viewpoint	11.9%	11.4%	13.7%
Deal directly with key decision makers	11.6	11.4	12.6
Use data to convince others	11.4	10.5	10.9
Form alliances and coalitions	9.4	7.5	17.1
Focus on target group	9.2	8.0	6.9
Use personal attributes	7.3	5.8	4.6
Be persistent	7.0	7.1	2.9
Work around roadblocks	5.8	5.9	4.6
Use contacts for information	5.8	6.7	4.0
Surround oneself with competent others	5.4	5.1	3.4
Use organizational rules	4.9	4.6	1.7
Commit uncommitted	3.0	4.8	2.3
Exaggerate information	2.0	2.0	4.6
Deal with others socially	1.3	2.9	2.9
Discredit opposition	1.4	1.5	1.1
Give guarantees	1.0	3.0	1.1
Offer favors/monetary rewards	0.8	0.9	2.9
Use threats	0.8	0.9	2.3

and the interview methodologies, and across two cultures. The five most frequently mentioned strategies by the U.S. managers and the U.K. managers on the questionnaire are the same as those selected by the U.S. managers in the original interview study. The "bottom rung" of strategies used least frequently was also similar across the two different cultures and the two research methodologies: use threats, give guarantees, offer favors, and discredit the opposition.

For the most part, the power strategies used most frequently, such as be persistent, were commonly regarded as socially acceptable approaches for influencing others. Only a minority of managers used threats, offered bribes, or criticized the competition to get their way. These results address a major misconception about power strategies, which typically tend to be associated with subversive, negative activities.

Strategies for Success

Are certain strategies more likely to be linked with successful rather than unsuccessful outcomes? A statistical analysis selected those strategies more frequently used in successful than unsuccessful situations.

As shown in Table 4–4, the successful strategies fall primarily into three broad categories, which we labeled: *using social networks, playing it straight,* and *going around the formal system.* The first group, *using social networks,* includes strategies that: form alliances and coalitions; deal directly with key decision makers; and use contacts for information. The second category, *playing it straight,* includes actions that: use data to convince others; be persistent; and focus on needs of target group. The third category, *going around the formal system,* includes work around roadblocks and (don't) use organizational rules. (The latter strategy was stated on the questionnaire as use organizational rules, and when it was used, the results were frequently unsuccessful.) Interestingly, U.S. managers tended to employ a greater number and range of successful strategies than U.K. managers.

We were surprised to find that the most frequently used

Table 4–4
Strategies for Success

	U.S. Managers[1]	
	Successful	Unsuccessful
Using Social Networks		
• Alliances and coalitions	57%	30%
• Deal directly with key decision makers	60%	48%
• Contacts for information	32%	21%
Playing It Straight		
• Using data to convince others	59%	46%
• Focus on needs of target group	47%	36%
• Be persistent	39%	26%
Going Around the Formal System		
• Work around roadblocks	36%	18%
• Use organizational rules	16%	29%
	U.K. Managers[1]	
• Alliances and coalitions	61%	38%
• Use organizational rules	21%	41%

[1]The strategies shown here represent only those that revealed a statistically significant difference between the successful percentage and the unsuccessful percentage.

strategy reported in Table 4–3, present a persuasive viewpoint, does not appear in Table 4–4 as a successful strategy. We surmise that being persuasive in one's presentation style must be accompanied by more powerful strategies if the recipient is actually to be persuaded. Simply being articulate and smooth in one's delivery is not enough.

Ironically, even those strategies leading to success can also lead to failure. The most successful strategy, deal directly with key decision makers, was also used fairly often in unsuccessful situations. Therefore, there is substantial risk inherent in any strategy. We suspect that lack of success in using a potentially successful strategy may be caused by relying exclusively on that strategy, or by not having a sufficient power base to support the chosen strategy. For example, if one attempts a strategy of using data to convince others, that person should also focus on needs of the target group and have a strong power base of expertise, information, and political access.

The following case examples, based on voices from the interviews, reveal how managers pursued multiple strategies, accompanied by a variety of power bases.

Using Alliances

The utility of a coalition is illustrated in the case of Wayne, who is treasurer and controller of a Fortune 500 consumer goods company. After eighteen years with the same company, he wanted to establish an offshore trading company and felt the time was right for such a venture. He discussed how he brought his idea to fruition.

> It was most important for me to convince my company's president of the viability of this idea. I have expertise in this area and my reputation as a winner is well known. I decided that if I could parlay these two assets into gaining the support of others, then the total package would sell to the two top people.
>
> I personally visited all of the division vice presidents overseas, ostensibly to seek support for the project. In my discussions with each of them, I stressed the innovative aspects of the project. I implied that the trading company would be established and hinted strongly that their support would make them part of a successful project.
>
> Soon after I returned, I gave a formal presentation to the president, emphasizing the benefits of the project. I also stressed the strong support given to the project by the vice presidents of all the subsidiaries. I was given the go-ahead to establish the offshore trading company.

We see here how Wayne was able to develop a supportive network of top executives and then go directly to the key decision maker. Behind these strategies were power bases of reputation, expertise, and political access.

A Board Member Blocks an Idea

The power of gaining support from others to prevent a decision is demonstrated in the case of Thomas, who sits on the board of directors, and was former chairman, of a medium-sized bank. He had been with the bank since college graduation. According to Thomas:

> While I was chairman, there was a move afoot to get the bank to sponsor a real estate investment trust. The bank would profit from this, but the investors might not fair as well. All the board members were in favor of the idea but I did not think it was right for our bank to sponsor it.
>
> First, I appealed to the board members' conscience in a formal presentation. Then I spoke individually to each member. Finally, I walked into the next meeting, pounded my fist on the table, and flatly stated that it would not be done while I was chairman.
>
> Someone else might have looked like a fool. But I knew I would get strong support from a lot of influential people. I sit on the boards of twenty organizations, and most are customers of this bank. These alliances, coupled with my successful accomplishments here over the last forty-six years, did the trick. I blocked the idea.

Unlike Wayne, who had to create a coalition from scratch, Thomas appealed to a social network built up over many years. His power bases were tradition, reputation, others' support, and charisma.

Do Not Go by the Book

Managers in both the U.S. and U.K. said that going by the book and following the chain of command are not very effective ways to get things done. Using organizational rules was a strategy more likely to be applied in unsuccessful influence attempts than in successful ones.

Jane, the publications coordinator described earlier in this chapter, presented an example illustrating the folly of going by the book.

> We put out a placement brochure every spring. I am in charge of deciding, with supervisory approval, how many should be printed. Several years ago a director of one of our divisions wanted to increase the size of the printing order. We discussed his reasons. I did not agree with him and decided to keep the original order. He seemed displeased, but didn't say any more to me.
>
> I submitted my order request to my boss. A week later, much to my surprise, I was told my order must be changed. A larger quantity was necessary.
>
> Later on I found out that the director had aligned with another director, convincing him that a larger order was extremely important this year. Both went to my supervisor and convinced her of the necessity of such a large order.
>
> Needless to say, I learned about getting things done, the hard way. The next year, before I submitted my request, I made sure that the two influential directors agreed with my decision. I showed them the costs and how many were left over from the previous year. And sure enough, each let their approval be known informally to my boss.

Persistence Pays Off

The research study also underscores the importance of *playing it straight* when trying to get things accomplished. The three strategies within this category, use data to convince others, be persistent, and focus on target group, tend to result in success.

Ed, manager of human resource development in a consumer goods company, illustrates such an approach. He found just the right person for his newly created slot of research associate. Mary had impeccable credentials. She was from a top applied psychology program and her references were excellent. Mary's prior work experience was in developing entrepreneurs for strategic business units (SBUs), and that was just what Ed wanted. But Ed's boss, Arthur, didn't see her in the same light. "She's a psychologist who wants to analyze our managers, she doesn't understand business."

But Ed persisted with Arthur. He said, "Let's just have her over for a brief interview. We don't have to commit ourselves." Prior to Mary's visit, he gathered more data about her work on SBUs and showed it to Arthur, along with another copy of her resume. He also arranged for a well-respected senior executive, with SBU experience, to interview Mary and write a brief review. Arthur was impressed with Mary but still uncertain. At that point, Ed presented the senior executive's positive evaluation, along with a *Wall Street Journal* article on the need for more research on entrepreneurs. Ed's persistence and use of data paid off. Arthur not only agreed to hire Mary, but he said, "She is just what we are looking for."

Linking Power Bases with Strategies

Power strategies are closely related to power bases. If you have not got the power base, then you cannot use the strategy effectively. The previous cases illustrate this relationship. In blocking the real estate trust, Thomas, the bank chairman, pounded his fist on the table, stating, "This won't be done while I am chairman." As he recognized, without a strong power base of reputation and others' support, such a dramatic and arbitrary position would have appeared ludicrous, even given his position power.

Table 4–5 shows how the strategies for success categories conceptually relate to the power base categories. The first general category of *playing it straight,* and its accompanying strategies, usually depends on supporting knowledge power bases of expertise, information, or tradition. For example, Ned, the corporate planner, needed a power base founded in expertise and information to pursue his strategy of using data to convince others about the validity of market segmentation. The publications coordinator, Jane, also used expertise and information to implement her

Table 4–5
Power Base and Power Strategy Connection

Individual Power Bases	Strategies for Success
Knowledge	*Playing It Straight*
• Expertise	• Use data to convince
• Information	• Focus on target group
• Tradition	• Be persistent
Others' Support	*Using Social Networks*
• Political access	• Alliances and coalitions
• Staff support	• Deal with decision maker
	• Contacts for information
Personality	*Going Around Formal System*
• Charisma	• Work around roadblocks
• Reputation	• (Don't) use organization rules
• Professional credibility	

strategy of focusing on needs of the target group in getting her design team selected.

The second power strategies category, *using social networks,* builds off the power bases of political access and staff support. Ned, the corporate planner, needed political access to get in the CEO's door with his strategy of appealing to key decision makers. And Jane ingeniously created a power base of staff support in putting her allies on the selection team, which in turn supported her in dealing directly with the vice dean.

The final strategies category of *going around the formal system* often requires a power base founded in personality, such as reputation, charisma, or professional credibility. Ned used his reputation as a winner to work around roadblocks thrown up by arguments against his plan. And Wayne, the treasurer and controller, also built off his reputation base to step outside the chain of command in seeking support from the division vice presidents.

This conceptual linkup of power strategies and bases should not be followed as if it were an inflexible recipe for success. That would belie the complexity of using power and influence flexibly to meet the needs of each situation. Most of the examples demonstrate how power bases flowing from personality served to fuel strategies in all three success categories. Combinations of several power bases can add greater weight to a particular strategy, such as Jane used in combining expertise, staff support, and professional credibility to convince the vice dean.

Selecting a Strategy

We should recognize by now that power strategies are more than a series of tricks to be used as if they were magic. The successful use of a given strategy depends not only on supporting power bases but also on other situational factors: (1) the power bases of others; (2) time perspective; and (3) personal style.

Power Bases of Others

Assessing the power bases of those people you are trying to influence is essential. If both parties have similar power bases, such as expertise and information, then it would be unwise to pursue the single strategy of *playing it straight,* since that strategy is likely available to the other party. The net result would probably be active combat that could end in a draw.

One alternative approach is to develop an additional base of power that your opponent does not possess. One manager of an internal consulting and research group was trying to influence another in-house research group to use a questionnaire in a proposed joint project. Both groups had a power base of expertise. The first manager, however, had also cultivated political access with a key vice president. He presented his ideas to her beforehand. She liked his ideas and let her approval be known informally. At the final meeting, as head to head expertise strategies were getting nowhere, it was tacit approval by the key vice president that swung the decision in favor of the manager of the consulting and research group.

Time Perspective

The old adage that timing is everything seems particularly true in choosing when to apply a certain strategy. The advantages of long-term success versus short-term failure must be considered. It may be, in the long run, more productive to lose the battle but win the war.

The best advice regarding timing comes from Machiavelli, who observes:

> If a man behaves with patience and circumspection and the time and circumstances are such that this method is called for, he will prosper; but if time and circumstance change, he will be ruined because he does not change his policy. . . . Men prosper as long as fortune and policy are in accord. . . . (pp. 132, 133)

Such advice was not followed in one case that we uncovered in our research. The staff members in the office of the secretary of a large nonprofit organization had final approval over all written policies and procedures for the organization. However, they were constantly complaining that no one took them seriously. The department head decided to make the approval process more difficult. He wanted his office to be right in every situation, and consequently, it rarely compromised, even on minor points of disagreement. They used a power strategy of persistence, pounding away until they won on every point. In the short run, they were victorious. But in the long run, many departments stopped sending them policies or even responding to their memos. Most of the organization viewed them as a pain in the neck, to be circumvented if possible. The department's original power base of centrality in the approval process had been eroded by other groups finding ways around the system.

Personal Style

Power strategies are like clothes; some outfits look better on some people than others. When long skirts and large hats are in vogue, short women will still stick to styles that are more appropriate to their shorter proportions.

Similarly, not all strategies work well for all people. Some people are extremely effective using power strategies that are "up front," such as deal directly with key decision makers. Others achieve more success with more discrete behind-the-scenes strategies, such as alliances and coalitions. One's personal style, therefore, becomes an important factor in choosing a particular power strategy.

A director of a state agency had continuing success with his behind-the-scenes style. In one situation, he wanted to be appointed to a national traveling committee. So he publicized the solid productivity record of his department. He also made speeches, stating that only the best leaders should be sent on this important visitation. Yet he never once suggested that he was interested in the committee appointment. He was appointed.

The same director acted similarly at a later point when seeking another agency position. Hearing through the grapevine that his own agency might be disbanded, he began to visit other agencies. He socialized with people in power and actively discussed his prior accomplishments. When an opening occurred in one of the larger agencies, he was immediately identified as the top choice. During the entire process, he never mentioned that he was interested in another job.

Implications for OD

The research data presented in this chapter illustrate that having a power base is not enough to influence others. We must also be competent in selecting and using certain power strategies that are consistent with our power bases and the situation at hand. OD consultants are no different from practicing managers in this regard. They need to develop power strategies for implementing change that fit not only with their power bases but with how other managers gain influence in their organizations. OD will rarely sell itself on its own merits.

Pettigrew (1975) and Schein (1977b) have long advocated the acquisition of power strategies by OD consultants. Yet many OD advocates resist this advice because such maneuvers appear inconsistent with OD's long-espoused values of trust and openness. We hope such assumptions are dispelled in this chapter, by cases in which many of the reported successful strategies do not, in fact, seem inconsistent with OD's basic values.

The power strategies immediately available to OD grow naturally out of its traditional knowledge bases of expertise and information. These strategies fall into the *playing it straight* category, where using data to convince others, being persistent, and focusing on needs of the target group can lead to greater influence. Successful application of these strategies can, in turn, build additional power bases of reputation and professional credibility.

It has been less common for OD to pursue power strategies related to *using social networks* or *going around the formal system*. OD practitioners may not feel comfortable in pursuing these less than "up front" strategies. However, in the application of these strategies, OD is more likely to come in contact with and be accepted by key decision makers.

Deciding not to shy away from the bottom line values advocated by executives who put business first is important for OD consultants in establishing alliances and gradually forming a power base of political access. We have seen OD consultants team up with a well-regarded line executive for whom a successful project was completed, and then jointly approach top management with an expanded proposal, using "bottom-line" data from the previous project to win acceptance.

5

Deceiving Others Through Power: All That Glitters . . .

Where in this discussion of power in organizations are the manipulators, the back stabbers, and those who profit at the expense of others? Do "differing objectives," bywords in the Pluralistic/Political model, simply mask unsavory aspects of behavior? More importantly, can we work with the realities of power in organizations and still sort out deceit from honest efforts?

The Pluralistic/Political model takes a broad and understanding view of power. It recognizes differing objectives among managers, and it accepts conflict as a natural outcome of these differences. Expressions of power often reflect honest differences between people seeking to achieve their work-related objectives. This political viewpoint is not so quick as OD to slap negative labels of selfishness or Machiavellianism or win–lose on all expressions of power.

Accepting the realities and necessities of power in organizations, however, does not negate the fact that "all that glitters is not gold." There is a cloak and dagger aspect to power that must be considered. The purpose of this chapter is to examine the *what, why, how,* and *where* of deceptive behavior in organizations. In doing so, we will consider the functionality of deception; is it always negative?

Defining Deception

What do clowns, the CIA, actors, business people, and court room defendants all have in common? All use some form of deception, at times, to achieve their objectives. These various groups were brought together at a 1976 Conference on Deception sponsored by the U.S. Department of Defense in the hopes of understanding better the concept of deception. Each group presented and discussed how they worked; these presentations included magic tricks, spying equipment, lie detector tests, and more academic types of analyses.

Out of this diverse group of people and activities emerged a definition of deception. *Deceptive behaviors are those actions intended to create a false impression of reality.* What you see is not what is really happening. What is being expressed masks an entirely different emotion. What is being requested is not really what is desired. In most cases, a clever illusion masks a different reality. OD speaks of this behavior in terms of the *hidden agenda.*

Machiavelli, in giving advice to his Prince, spoke openly of the importance of deception. He indicated that creating an illusion of being honest, compassionate, and generous is important to gaining and maintaining power. Yet, so too is the necessity of breaking one's word, being cruel, and being parsimonious. "Be a lion and a fox," was his advice.

A cursory look at behavior in organizations suggests that Machiavelli is still active among us, doling out advice. His ghostly hand would seem to have scripted a memo that distorts or omits information; his spirit would seem to have encouraged meetings to be held to decide what has already been decided, or rewards to be promised but never given out.

During our field interviews, we discovered a manager who was opposed to any kind of change, but he covered this up with endless studies that caused actions to be deferred or even forgotten. There was also a senior executive who gave the appearance of selecting successors on the basis of competency. In reality, he was selecting people on the basis of loyalty and conformity to his image and ideas. There were several managers who created the illusion of being favorable toward participative decision making, yet guided their subordinates to an outcome predetermined by themselves.

Deceptive behaviors are an active component of organizational life. They range from the harmless to the harmful. At times, these illusions produce minor victories, such as a vote deferred or a report postponed. At other times, deception can result in promotions lost or project approvals overturned.

Two Sides of Power

Why do these deceptions occur? What prompts such actions? Answers can be found by examining more closely the intent of the person choosing to exercise power over another individual or group. Why is he or she choosing to modify the behaviors of others? What are his or her objectives?

Broadly speaking, an individual's intents can be categorized as either *work-related* or *self-oriented* (Schein, 1977a). It is the self-oriented intents that promote deception, and thereby allow us to understand why "all that glitters" is not what it seems to be.

Work-related power behaviors are those actions designed to get one's job done in an organization. It is the expression of power by those seeking to fulfill their work-related objectives. The bulk of the discussion and examples in Chapters 2, 3, and 4 focus on these types of work-related behaviors. Jack, the financial director, used power to get his projects implemented in his chemical company. The superintendent in the steel company needed power to get a more efficient delivery schedule of slabs. Wayne, the treasurer and controller, exercised power to successfully establish an offshore trading company. In all cases, the effective use of power was essential in getting the job done.

Not all expressions of power, however, relate to the process of getting work done. Also present within organizations are power strategies designed solely to promote selfish objectives. Highly personalized objectives such as promotion, money, status, and job survival can dominate individual behavior more than work-related objectives.

The key distinction between self-oriented and work-related intents lies in the priority of the person exercising power. Self-oriented behavior is just that — pursuit of self-aggrandizement — regardless of the work-related effects. Managers whose political behaviors are focused primarily on getting the job done may indeed be aware of personal gain, but that is not their primary intent.

The actions of Tom, the head of a production unit, illustrate how self-oriented intents may override work-related objectives. He pushed his people and equipment hard, resulting in dramatic efficiencies in production. The results were highly visible and, in short order, Tom was promoted. Much later it appeared that Tom's push for short-term efficiency did serious damage to the work unit. Productivity declined to a level even lower than when Tom first headed the unit. What happened? Tom's intent was strictly personal: he wanted to get a promotion. He knew that highly visible and fast results would achieve this objective. He was not concerned with long-term negative effects. He also knew the company well enough to realize that, by the time lower productivity became evident, it would be unlikely that he would be connected with the downturn.

Going Undercover

There is usually a direct link between one's intent and the overt versus covert nature of one's behaviors. If the intent is self-oriented, the power expression is likely to be covert. Typically, organizationally sanctioned activities are used to cover up the underlying motive. The overt legitimate action overlays the covert set of intents. The illusion of a company orientation masks the reality of behaviors designed to achieve personal objectives.

What follows are two real-life examples of power situations where personal intents are given top priority. Each person uses an overt set of organizationally sanctioned intents and strategies to disguise a personal set of intents and strategies.

Discrediting a Research Group

Sally is the director of branch office research in a large financial institution. Within this company, there is a sister research unit, corporate research. Both are similar in size and position in the hierarchy. Their main difference is the population toward which each unit's efforts are applied.

Sally discovered that corporate research is about to receive approval to do a large study of a computer operation in the corporate office. She feels threatened by a large-scale research endeavor; perhaps her own unit will appear inadequate or her own abilities will be questioned. Her position, she believes, will be seriously undermined in the eyes of the organization if the other research unit successfully carries out the project.

Sally's self-oriented intent is to maintain her own power in research expertise. Her hidden strategy is to discredit the other research group and block the project. She cannot, of course, reveal this intent or strategy. So, using her power bases of expertise and tradition — she once worked in computer operations — she establishes an overt strategy by asking to review the project.

Sally's covert strategy, however, is quite different. After reviewing the report, she prepares a memo raising several questions about the adequacy of the methodology used in the study, coupled with references to her knowledge of computer operations. She sends a copy of this memo to the corporate research director and to other interested parties in the organization, including the common boss of the two research directors.

Sally's initial strategy is successful. The director responds to the memo, allowing Sally further opportunity to reply in writing. She brings up even more questions and sends out a further round of memos. Sally's plan is to confuse the issue, planting seeds of doubt about the competency of the corporate research unit. If she is successful, final approval for the research project will be delayed or even rescinded. At the same time, she appears, on the surface, to be sincerely interested in improving an important research project.

Plotting for Promotion

Gary is the ambitious manager of Equal Employment Opportunity in a large communications company. He proposes to develop a large training program, with several additional staff members under his direction, to improve the status of women in the company. He has reputational and expertise power from his

EEO work in another company. Gary's proposal wins out over one submitted by the corporate training department. Unfortunately, Gary's personal intent has little to do with equality for women; instead, he wants a promotion with higher pay outside the EEO group. If his assessment of the company is correct, increasing the number of people who report directly to him will lead to a higher level managerial position. He covers up his covert intent with an overt one of improving the status of women in the company.

High Cost of Deception

Dealing with deceptive activities can be quite confusing to the person on the receiving end. The director of corporate research must have been exasperated by Sally's questions regarding the computer project. Cancellation of the project would come as a very unpleasant and unexpected outcome. Moreover, Sally may have stalled or prevented a research endeavor with potentially valuable outcomes to the organization. The EEO training program implemented by Gary's group may well have been needed in the company. However, the price the company paid was inflated by Gary's salary increase and by a substantial growth in staff that actually replicated an already existing staff in the corporate training department.

High and Low Slack Systems

Is there a way to determine if the reality of political behavior is really an illusion? Why do self-oriented intents and deceptive behaviors persist in organizations? Can they be eradicated? There are no easy answers to these questions. However, one way to deal with them is to consider deceptive behavior as most frequently evident in *high slack* organizations.

Organizations can be dichotomized into either *high* or *low slack systems* (Cyert and March, 1964). High slack systems are those organizations operating with an abundance of resources in reasonably stable and minimally competitive environments. Participants focus on routine activities in order to operate efficiently. Low slack systems are those operating in highly competitive environments that require rapid and nonroutine decision making. A high level of productive energy and innovation is required if the system is to remain effective.

A decade ago banks and insurance companies were ideal examples of high slack companies. Maintaining order and routine within a minimally competitive business environment made for successful enterprises. Today a changing environment has forced many such organizations either to become low slack systems or to go out of business. AT&T can be characterized as a once high slack system now moving into a low slack mode of operation. Many government agencies are high slack systems. On the other hand, most computer companies, such as Apple and Compaq, are low slack organizations.

Given this distinction, the ratio of self-oriented to work-related intents appears to be greater in high slack systems, while the reverse is true in low slack systems (Schein, 1979). In low slack systems, vigorous competition in the environment prevents managers from easily tailoring their activities to achieve personal ends. Getting the work done and done well are paramount demands if people want to keep their jobs or advance in the company. There is little room, time, or opportunity for personal intents to flourish or be disguised as work-related behavior.

In high slack systems, on the other hand, the absence of intense competition permits managers to pursue personal goals without causing obvious disruption in the system. There is ample opportunity for project blocking, promotion plotting, or empire building — while successfully maintaining day-to-day operations.

High slack systems, then, are often a hotbed of deceptive activities that cover up the exercise of power for personal gain. Given the high cost and disruptive nature of such behaviors, an OD consultant might ask: "How can these dysfunctional behaviors be eliminated?" Such a question, however, may be asked too quickly. The presence of self-oriented political behavior also serves some positive functions within high slack systems, and these must be considered before deciding how or even if such behaviors should be eliminated.

Functionality of Deception

In high slack industries, even high level jobs are fairly routine, thereby prompting the need for excitement, sometimes through political warfare. Deception and intrigue add interest to an otherwise boring and static work environment. Moreover, high slack systems are usually based on tenure. Covert tactics, like empire building, provide important rewards during the long intervals that exist between formal rewards, such as promotions.

One of our interviews with a manager in a high slack company illustrates the functionality of political intrigue. Sam has held the same job, manager of claims, for fifteen years in an old line insurance company. The business was highly profitable because of a narrow market niche in which there was little competition. On the surface, Sam's job looked quite routine and lacking in challenge. Listening to him, though, we heard quite another story. "It's dog-eat-dog competition around here. You never know what's going to happen next. Someone is always trying to outmaneuver me for more money or to steal my people, or even my job title. Last week, in health claims, there was a coup and Jane found herself reporting to a former peer. You can't miss a meeting or not read all memos between the lines. Its go, go, go around here."

Political warfare fosters the illusion of an active system full of excitement and competition. The reality of a boring job never has to be faced. The illusion of excitement and activity keeps members involved; it provides rewards not ordinarily forthcoming in a stagnant and routine system. To reduce such deception without recognizing its functional aspects would be foolhardy. The same activities could easily resurface again.

The only way to bring about permanent change is to introduce new energizers and reward mechanisms to replace those activities created through deception and political intrigue. Sometimes this can be done; certain jobs can be made more challenging and intrinsically interesting, and financial incentives and promotions can be timed to work achievements. Unfortunately, such changes cannot readily be made in high slack systems because of the routine nature of many jobs. In these cases, attempts to minimize deception can have a detrimental impact. The loss of excitement and personal rewards provided by such activities could grind the organization to a halt.

Going from Low to High Slack

People who move from a low slack to a high slack system may be unprepared for the change in the ratio between self-oriented and work-related power behaviors. Lack of this awareness can have serious negative consequences.

Take, for example, the case of a young, dynamic executive from a small high tech company who becomes the CEO of a large, bureaucratic high slack company. What happens when she arrives in the new environment? Many of her leadership behaviors seen as productive in the low slack system prove ineffective in the high slack company. She fails to recognize that getting things done requires a different way of exercising power. To her, deception and intrigue appear petty, and she criticizes those who engage in it.

The winds of deception whirl around her, but the new leader persists, without success, in stressing work-related activities. Finally, those in power use their knowledge of the system, with all its deception and intrigue, to oust her.

Going from High to Low Slack

When organizations move from high slack to low slack, its members may be unaware of the different types of power behavior expected of them. Savings and loan institutions, for example, were once high slack systems, and appropriately so in a regulated industry. Following deregulation and increasing competition, these institutions were forced to move toward low slack methods of operating.

In one of the deregulated Baby Bell companies, the human resources department was cut from sixty-five members to forty in just one year. One of the survivors made this comment to us: "All the people who couldn't adjust by showing they could perform additional jobs are gone. We had too many specialists who all looked busy but most of their time was spent writing memos and going to meetings."

Under such rapid changes, many managers often persist in their self-oriented power behavior. However, these actions prove disruptive to the efficient functioning of the new system. There is little room, time, or opportunity to play games for personal gain.

Implications for OD

The other side of power — deception for self-oriented objectives — is a force with which OD must contend. Otherwise, OD can itself be used by those seeking to fulfill their personal intents, even under the guise of constructive activities.

In one situation familiar to us, an OD consultant was asked to assess a conflict between two departments. The sponsor, a senior vice president in charge of both groups, appeared to be genuinely interested in resolving the conflict. In reality, OD was serving as a benign cover for a "hatchet job" on one of the department VPs. The senior VP manipulated the situation and even the results in order to expose the inadequacies of the marked VP. The OD consultant was an unwitting pawn in the senior VP's self-oriented power game.

OD should also consider being more strategic around the issue of openness. Sometimes, it may be more effective to withhold one's overall plan and reveal one's objectives slowly. One OD consultant, for example, wanted to conduct a company-wide employee attitude survey, but his client seemed reluctant to share the results beyond his own office. Instead of pressing for the large survey, the consultant suggested that a limited survey be taken in one department only, with the feedback confined to the client and the top management team in the surveyed department. The client agreed and, because the consultant involved the sponsoring executive in all aspects of the planning and feedback process, his fears and resistance were gradually allayed. The client subsequently supported a large-scale action/research project throughout the company.

On the other hand, sometimes a direct approach may be more appropriate. Why, for example, pretend that an OD program instituted and directed from the top is voluntary? Employees are rarely fooled; transparent deception can result in cynicism and lower commitment.

OD needs to keep in mind the different power behaviors spawned by high and low slack systems. Unless new energizers and rewards are introduced into high slack systems, attempts to eliminate deception and intrigue may be seriously resisted. Once, when we were using the high/low slack framework in a presentation to a senior executive group moving from high to low slack, one of its members excitedly said, "Now I know why Jack is still behaving the way he is!" Several others laughingly agreed, but the remainder of the session was spent in a serious discussion of what approach to take in assisting many old line executives to adjust to the new work environment.

Finally, OD needs to teach managers more about the constructive and deceptive sides of political behavior in organizations. Too often OD's educational content is confined to an idealized treatment of leadership behavior, in which the objective is a win-win solution. Experienced managers are not likely to be convinced by such a superficial treatment of the political reality facing them in everyday decision making.

6

Personalizing Power

People differ in their desire to use power for influencing others. Some feel comfortable with power, others do not. Some use it constructively and others abuse it. The effectiveness with which President Franklin Roosevelt dealt with power contrasts sharply with President Jimmy Carter's ambivalence toward power and his relative ineffectiveness in using it.

The popular press on power and influence tends to steer the public away from individual differences, stressing instead the viewpoint that anyone can do it. For example, books such as Michael Korda's *Power* (1975) suggest that just the knowledge that there exists a variety of power strategies and tactics is a sufficient basis for anyone to make successful influence attempts. These books feed on the public's need to feel more powerful, but simplistic checklists, composed of the "ten steps to becoming more powerful," overlook the complexity of personality differences.

Another popular book, Michael Maccoby's *The Gamesman* (1976), comes closer to recognizing individual differences. It classifies four types of organizational members: the Craftsman, the Company Man, the Jungle Fighter, and the Gamesman. In this classification scheme, the Craftsman has little desire to influence others, the Company Man is inhibited and fearful of using power, and the Jungle Fighter is an overt and crass user of power. Maccoby's ideal for today's organizations is the Gamesman, who achieves personal objectives through subtle timing and persuasion, often in group settings.

Maccoby's analysis suggests that not all individuals have the same innate ability, appropriate background, or motivation to influence others. His scheme implies that a checklist approach would probably be ignored by the Craftsman, used ineffectually by the Company Man, and abused by the Jungle Fighter. The Gamesman would not need a checklist at all.

Beyond popular treatments of power, several different frameworks can be drawn from the scholarly literature for understanding better the relationship between power and personality. We will examine closely three different approaches: the empirical measurement of need for power and Machiavellianism, psychoanalytic interpretation, and the role of social learning in childhood.

The Power Motive

One empirical approach to understanding power and personality is to measure an individual's need for power. Winter (1973) found that individuals with a high need for power tend to hold offices in organizations and use power strategies such as gaining visibility, forming alliances, acting competitively, and valuing prestige. He also found that individuals with a high need for power are attracted to occupations that offer an opportunity to use power and influence, such as business management.

Similarly, McClelland and Burnham (1976) discovered that male managers scored higher on the need for power than did men in general. In addition, the power motive was correlated with managerial effectiveness, as measured by subordinates' ratings of organizational clarity and team spirit. Other researchers have shown similar positive relationships between the need for power and managerial success (Cummin, 1965; Lennerlof, 1967). McClelland and Burnham also observe that the power motive is more indicative of managerial success than the achievement motive, the latter being more closely associated with entrepreneurs.

In a further breakdown of the power motive, McClelland

divided people with a high need for power into two types: personal power managers and institutional power managers. Personal power managers tend to elicit loyalty to themselves rather than the organization. The institutional power managers place the good of the company over self-interest. The institutional power manager believes in centralized authority, in the discipline of work, has a keen sense of justice, and feels that a person who works hard and sacrifices for the organization will be rewarded for his or her efforts. There is a close connection here between McClelland's personal and institutional managers and our self-oriented and work-related managers described in Chapter 5.

The Machiavellian Scale

Another useful and enlightening approach to measuring personality differences in the use of power was developed by Christie and Geis in their book, *Studies in Machiavellianism* (1975). They designed a scale to measure people on their attitudes toward Machiavellianism and then conducted a variety of field and experimental studies to determine the behavioral characteristics of those who scored high (High Machs) and those who scored low (Low Machs) on the scale. Although their research population was confined to college students, the findings reveal significant behavioral differences between the two groups.

High Machs agree with Machiavellian statements such as, "Anyone who completely trusts anyone else is asking for trouble," while Low Machs are more likely to agree with statements such as, "It is possible to be good in all respects." High Machs are characterized as "cool"; more likely to resist social influence; have an orientation toward ideas rather than people; and are more likely to initiate and control a structured environment. On the other hand, Low Machs are classified as being a "soft touch"; more likely to be susceptible to social influence; have an orientation to people rather than ideas; and are more likely to accept and follow a structured environment.

In situations where competition is involved, High Machs are more likely to win if there is face-to-face interaction, latitude for improvisation, and some degree of *irrelevant affect* (for example, when a third party breaks into tears for no apparent reason). Low Machs are easily disrupted by irrelevant emotional factors. High Machs reflect a greater emotional detachment in general.

High Machs are better able to adapt their tactics to the particular situation; Low Machs become engrossed in the other individuals' needs, while neglecting their own needs. High Machs appear just as aware of others' needs as Low Machs, but the former are more likely to use this information to benefit themselves in striking a bargain with the other person.

We can surmise from these characteristics that High Machs are likely to be more comfortable with and successful at exercising power. Strategies such as dealing directly with key decision makers, being persistent, focusing on needs of the target group, and working around roadblocks are more High Mach than Low Mach approaches to dealing with others.

Christie and Geis also sought to find out *why* people differ on the Machiavellian scale. Interestingly, there is a striking lack of relationship between Mach scores and demographic characteristics. No differences exist between High and Low Machs in IQ or education. High Machs are as likely to be found among the underprivileged as those people with high social status. They also found Machiavellianism in children as young as ten years old.

According to Christie and Geis (p. 338),

> There are no hard data indicating causes of individual differences, but they are clearly not related to the social status of the parents. It is suggested that some manipulative behaviors are learned at an early age by being rewarded unintentionally by parents and by early exposure to nonfamilial socializing agents such as peers and mass media. The one sure conclusion is that marked individual differences in Machiavellianism are attributable to a very complex social learning process, and that the parameters have not yet been clearly identified.

Psychoanalytic Perspective

Although the psychoanalytic school is not concerned directly with the measurement of personality and power, it does provide clues about the unconscious motivations behind varying power behaviors. For the most part, this viewpoint considers power behavior a neurotic manifestation of unresolved conflicts stemming from inconsistent childhood experiences, such as a desire to please one's father; rebellion against parental figures; desire to overcome parental authority; fear of punishment; or fear of expressing genuine emotion.

Zaleznik (1970), and Zaleznik and Kets de Vries in *Power and the Corporate Mind* (1975), analyze corporate behavior from this psychoanalytic perspective. Zaleznik presents three "life dramas" intertwined with varying expressions of power. One drama portrays stripping power from a parental figure, such as in the overthrow of a CEO. In 1975, Robert Sarnoff was ousted from his lofty position as CEO of RCA and the plotters in this corporate coup d'etat were insiders.

A second life drama portrays the predominance of paranoid thinking, reflected in mistrust, suspicion, and jealousy. The dramatic ouster of Lew Glucksman as managing partner at prestigious Lehman Brothers, and the subsequent demise of the firm, suggest a playing out of this life drama (Auletta, 1986). Glucksman came from a less socially and educationally acceptable background than his Ivy League colleagues, so to compensate he did everything possible to demean them once he had maneuvered himself into power. Grandiose ideas and an overestimation of one's power and abilities, such as in the case of Jimmy Hoffa or John DeLorean, causes corporate leaders to act as if they are omnipotent, sometimes leading to unfortunate outcomes.

A third life drama portrays a ritualistic ceremony in which power issues are submerged by compulsive behavior, at the cost of real problem solving. A CEO may engage several consultants and hold regular off-site retreats—all of which appear to provide a forum for openly solving problems. In reality, however, these activities mask the CEO's real need to deny conflicts by keeping people appeased. Zaleznik makes an interesting distinction between two types of power alignments among people at work. There are coalitions that represent the aggregation of power with the conscious intent of using members' abilities for constructive purposes. And there are collusions, which reflect a predominance of unconscious conflict and defensive behavior. In the latter instance, we find a subordinate who is sensitive to the unconscious desires of his superior, such as a need for admiration and loyalty. The subordinate and superior then align with each other in mutual satisfaction of their unconscious needs. The subordinate provides admiration and loyalty, and the superior bestows rewards in return.

In a further application of psychoanalytic thinking to the negative effects of power dynamics at the top on unsuccessful organizations, Kets de Vries and Miller (1984) identify five neurotic organizational styles: Paranoid, Compulsive, Dramatic, Depressive, and Schizoid.

The Schizoid organization is characterized by a leadership vacuum at the top: the CEO fears personal involvement, becomes withdrawn, is insecure, and refuses to adopt consistent policies. This behavior results in the second-tier management becoming a political arena for those seeking to win favor from an unresponsive leader. Strategy making resides in a shifting coalition of aspiring middle managers who try to woo an indecisive leader by advancing their own projects.

In the Paranoid organization, senior management's mistrust and suspicion toward the outside world is translated by management into an emphasis on organizational intelligence and control. The Compulsive organization reflects top management's obsessive need to reduce internal uncertainty by establishing rigid controls, a steep hierarchy relying on position power, and strict compliance with procedures and standards. The Dramatic organization also centralizes power at the top, but here it is done by the CEO to gain visibility as he or she takes center stage by fostering boldness, risk taking, and unbridled growth. The Depressive organization reflects a power vacuum at the top because senior management sees the course of events as unalterable; hence, the organization assumes a conservative, bureaucratic, and passive tone.

We learn from the psychoanalytic school to understand more about the destructive side of power, and especially how unresolved power issues can deeply disturb and even corrupt not only top management but an entire organization. Many managers obviously seek power for deep-seated reasons, and when they have it, their unique expression of it can cause destructive dynamics that may eventually destroy an organization.

_____

Social Learning in Childhood

Despite the utility of psychoanalytic thinking, it is misleading to think that all roots of power-oriented behavior have a pathologic basis. As suggested earlier by Christie and Geis, it may be that certain power behaviors are simply learned socially through our interaction with role models during childhood.

Doris Kearns (1976), in her analysis of Lyndon Johnson's political personality, relates Johnson's early childhood experiences to his later desire for power and the particular "power style" that characterized his political career. According to Kearns, Johnson's childhood was dominated by two parents with opposing sets of needs and wants. His mother stressed intellectual and cultural achievement, while his father considered intellect and culture to be unmanly. Each parent withheld or bestowed rewards for Johnson's accomplishments. Johnson rejected neither mother nor father; instead, he attempted constantly to reconcile and satisfy both parents' expectations.

Kearns relates these childhood conditions to parallels in Johnson's power style during his political career. In particular, she points out his keen ability to deal with contradictions. Johnson would often move in contradictory directions, yet he would usually achieve consensus. He had the ability to bargain by simultaneously trading favors while exercising a coercive appeal . . . "I have done this for you, now if you don't do this for me, I will withdraw support." It was his characteristic trait never to reveal everything to everyone.

All of Johnson's power style—dealing with contradictions, his bargaining nature, his controlling approach, and the overall deceptive quality of his actions—seem to relate to learning in childhood about how to appease both his mother and his father. He practiced these behaviors constantly over time until a unique power style emerged, one that allowed him to become extremely effective in legislative situations.

Many of our power styles probably stem from social learning, suggesting that we gradually incorporate those strategies that
are successful for us into our personalities. The manager who
continually forms coalitions perhaps learned at an early age to
align with others and seek their support in order to get things
done. As a child, he or she probably encountered many different
types of people, with different needs and objectives. To get his or
her own way meant he or she continually had to form alliances.
Other managers well versed in using a power base of reputation
may have enjoyed the privileged status of being an only child or
first born. Early successes, encouraged by cheering parents, lead
to further accomplishments. Soon this star quality spills over into
schoolwork, sports, and social events. From an early age, he or
she learns the power of building on reputation in getting one's
way.

Power Styles and Flexibility

Is there one best way to express power? Clearly, everything
we know about individual and situational differences suggests a
strong negative response. Yet given the strong influence of prior
experience on our personalities, how flexible can we expect
people to be?

Machiavelli and Kearns share a similar pessimism about
the changeability of power styles. Although recognizing that different situations require different strategies, Machiavelli did not
believe that man changed easily:

> Nor do we find . . . man shrewd enough to know how to
> adapt his policy; either . . . he cannot do otherwise than
> what is in character or . . . having always prospered by pro-
> ceeding one way, he cannot persuade himself to change. (p.
> 132)

Similarly, Kearns suggests it may be difficult for one to alter one's power strategies if the situation changes. She refers to
Johnson's effectiveness in the legislature where bargaining and
deception were useful qualities. But these same power behaviors
proved ineffective in handling the Vietnam War. Kearns states,

... the very qualities and experience that led to his political and legislative success were precisely those that now operated to destroy him. His tendency to resolve conflict instead of accepting it ... was responsible for his rise to power and his success in the senate ... [N]ow [it] led him to manipulate and orchestrate the political process in order to shape a formula that could accommodate both the Great Society and Vietnam. Years of experience in gaining and exercising power had taught Johnson that the leader could move in contradictory directions at the same time so long as he compartmentalized everything he did and kept his dealings with one group secret from those with the next. (pp. 401–402)

Most people are probably not as rigid as Machiavelli suggests or President Johnson was. Nor are we as flexible as we would like to be. Successful executives seem to be both aware of their more rigid or predominant styles, and of their need to adapt to changing situations. The effective use of new power strategies, albeit awkward at first, encourages their use in the future. In addition, managers can align themselves with those who have dominant power styles more appropriate to a new situation. The "up front" manager whose power base is reputation can join with the more covert coalition manager to achieve mutual objectives.

Implications for OD

There is much for OD to learn and be sensitive about when dealing with issues of personality and power in organizations. Trying to change organizations often strikes deeply at the psyches and identities of those managers who hold or want more power. Strong emotions are aroused but rarely expressed openly when one's personal and organizational power is threatened by change.

One clear guideline is to accept the likelihood that many managers will assess any OD intervention for what it means personally to them in terms of their power base. Interventions designed to reduce or redistribute managerial influence, by thwarting the power motive for certain managers, are likely to be strongly resisted. At the same time, those managers who want more power are likely to be strong supporters of change when they see themselves receiving greater power.

Working through these power issues becomes a primary topic for the astute OD consultant. Simply prescribing new participative leadership styles for all effective managers can do more harm than good. It may be possible, when in a process consultation mode, to make the power issue a legitimate topic for discussion in a group that does not clearly recognize how the power dynamic is being evidenced in their behavior. Other times, when the issue is too explosive, it may have to be discussed privately with individuals who need to become more self-aware or informed about what others are doing. There are limits, however, to process interventions about power. The astute consultant needs to accept the fact that interventions may have to be made to remove, transfer, and select new managers in order to break the destructive dynamic caused by obstructive and unbending individuals. To accomplish such actions will require a strong consultant power base and political access to senior executives.

Because power and personality are closely linked, it means that individuals will not change easily. Accommodations will have to be made by OD consultants in adapting to the power styles of key managers. The pairing of a Low Mach OD consultant and a High Mach client is probably fairly frequent. It is not surprising that OD consultants may find it hard for their ideas to be accepted, and end up feeling as if they had been "run over" by the client. The reverse arrangement can also pose problems for OD. A High Mach consultant can congratulate herself with an agreed upon proposal for a change program, but perhaps the soft touch Low Mach client was too easily influenced, thereby failing to give alternative strategies sufficient consideration.

We also need to assess the strengths and limitations of our power styles as OD consultants across different situations, especially those where, in the past, we have been effective and those where we have drawn a blank. Leading with a power style we are skilled at and most comfortable with is probably the best advice, but the consulting task inherently requires flexibility. Evolving stages in the consulting process—gaining client access, selling a project, making interventions, and eventually letting go—all require different power approaches, as we shall see more clearly in Chapter 12. We therefore need to experiment with our own power styles, as well as to include colleagues who have complementary power styles.

Part II
Integration of Power with Organization Development

7

Diagnosing Power

It is essential that the OD consultant develop his or her diagnostic skills to identify power and its behavioral manifestations in real organizations. Failure to do so can easily make the consultant a victim of political intrigue. The best planned change efforts can be undone by a coalition of powerful executives who want to protect the status quo.

The challenge in making an accurate diagnosis begins immediately when the consultant enters the organization. If the consultant has a sponsoring executive who lacks power, then other executives are unlikely to be receptive to beginning a dialogue about the merits of OD assistance. In one Fortune One Hundred company, we were invited to develop a proposal by the executive vice president of human resources, who had a large, plush office on the top floor of an imposing skyscraper. We spent many hours with him and his subordinates in developing the proposal, only to learn later that he lacked sufficient funds in his budget and could not persuade other executives to fund the project.

A thorough diagnosis of power also becomes critical in the design and conduct of an OD program. Answers must be sought to questions such as: Who from the organization has sufficient power to lend credibility to the design of the effort? Should it be an organization-wide program requiring commitment from all top managers, or should it be limited to a smaller segment of the organization because so much rivalry exists among top management?

Diagnosis as an Art

Diagnosing power in organizations is not an exact science. It is a finely tuned art that depends on the perceptive skills and sound judgment of the consultant. As seen in previous chapters, many factors come to bear on determining power, and these factors vary in relative weight from one organization to the next. In one company, power may be determined by *expertise* and *information*, while in another it is derived from *tradition* and *political access* to the CEO.

Power is rarely overtly visible; it is often very subtle in its various expressions. The more traditionally manifest signs of power, such as a big office at the top of a skyscraper, can be seriously misleading. The astute consultant must look for power—it will not stand out like stars on a general's shoulder. Furthermore, the consultant's mind is likely to be preoccupied with the substantive content of the client's problem, causing him or her to overlook subtle cues about power.

Any sign or symptom of power has to be recorded by the OD consultant. These signs need to be sifted through constantly, and frequent judgments must be made about the relative capacity of various parties, including the consultant's power, to influence the course of events. Such judgments are a synthetic human act, honed by constant practice and checked against the judgments of others.

Power Relationship Map

The question of *where* to look for power is the first priority in gathering data. We begin by looking at power *relationships*, not at the absolute power of any single individual. Although an individual or group may appear powerful along certain dimensions, such as formal authority, this assessment is meaningless unless compared against other individuals and groups in the organization.

Two basic relationships must be assessed initially: (1) the relative power between the OD consultant and the client sponsor with whom the consultant is dealing, and (2) the relative power between the sponsor and other key executives. If the consultant lacks the power to influence the sponsor or if the sponsor lacks the power to influence the organization, then no OD project will ever be initiated.

In most situations, however, the network of power relationships is much more complex than these two basic relationships. The map in Figure 7–1 identifies seven relationships that can affect the overall course of an OD effort.

We will briefly discuss each of these power relationships for their importance in making a comprehensive diagnosis.

1. *Consultant to Sponsor:* To gain access, the consultant must have influence over a key person in top management who is interested in furthering an OD effort. The consultant will need sufficient power to influence the sponsor in order to sell the effort to others in the organization. If the sponsor is indifferent to the consultant's presence and ideas, then consultant power is lacking.

2. *Sponsor to Other Key Executives:* Even if the consultant successfully influences the sponsor, rarely does the sponsor have the absolute power to force OD upon the organization. Other key executives have to be dealt with, and the sponsor may be at a power disadvantage with these executives.

3. *Key Executives to Each Other:* Although the sponsor may have the power to influence one or two key executives, there may be others in the top group who are resistant. The power dynamics among all of the top group needs to be assessed, especially if the OD project is to be organization-wide and implemented with full commitment from top management.

4. *Consultant to Key Executives:* Even if the sponsor lacks the power to influence other key executives, the consul-

tant may be able to fill that void. We have at times withdrawn tactfully from a weak sponsor to align with a
new sponsor who is more powerful.
5. *Top Executives to Higher Authority:* We have seen OD
efforts at the division level undermined by senior executives at the corporate level. So, even though a key decision maker authorizes an OD program at one level, it is
wise to look above to assess his or her power relationship with higher level executives.
6. *Key Executives to the Organization:* It may well be that
top management has abdicated much of its authority to
lower levels, and that lower levels do not respect top
management. Hence, even top management can lack
the power needed to implement an OD project and have
it accepted by the rest of the organization.
7. *Organizational Units to Each Other:* As we know from
Chapter 3, some departments have more power than
others in the organization. Thus, for example, if marketing in a consumer goods company has more power than
production, any OD program identified with production
will be swimming upstream in trying to exert influence
over marketing.

Power Dimensions

Now that we know *where* to look, we need to consider
what to look for in assessing and determining the relative weight
and character of various power relationships. The OD consultant
is seeking an overall assessment of each power relationship.

There are objective and subjective indicators of power. The
objective side can be found in tangibles such as organizational
charts and job descriptions; the subjective side exists more informally in the way people think about and act toward each other.
What people tell you about various individuals and how they act
toward each other can reveal much about who has power and who
does not. For example, although an organization chart may indi-
cate someone holds high rank and position power, in fact that
person's informal status and reputation power can be much

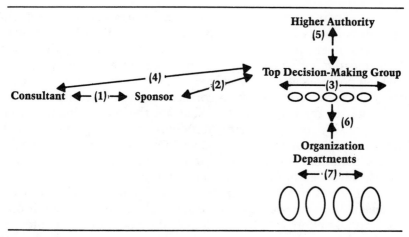

Figure 7-1
Key Power Relationships

lower. An organizational culture that values seniority and experience may attribute little power to a new executive with an exalted title of vice president and an M.B.A.

We start by assessing the individual power bases of senior and middle level executives. We note who has greater power based on a combination of *knowledge, personality,* and *others support.* Sometimes the salience of certain power bases may shift with topical issues. For instance, the senior research scientist who holds both a Ph.D. and several patents may be deferred to by top executives on technological questions, even though she is two levels down in the organization chart and ignored on other issues.

Next, department power bases should be considered. Which departments have the largest numbers of people and assets under their control? Which departments, even if small in size, are considered vital (*i.e., have centrality*) to the workings of the company. We recognized the power of a small research and development department in one company when we discovered that the CEO still retained a "second office" in the R&D laboratory.

The perceptive consultant should also be alert to the way power is distributed in the organization. Is it concentrated more at the top or is it widely delegated? An OD program designed to promote participative management in an organization in which power is tightly held at the top will not sit well with key power holders unless they are fully committed. Alternately, the same participative emphasis may be irrelevant in an organization in which power is already widely shared.

Another dimension to consider is the mode of power expression in the organization. What are the predominant power strategies? Is *playing it straight* a dominant strategy, which will make it easier for an OD consultant? Or is *using social networks* more common? Do coalitions tend to form frequently to get a cause advanced or opposed? Who belongs to these coalitions? Is there a lot of rivalry among key power holders or is there open respect? We have seen two powerful rivals in opposing coalitions use an OD effort as a political tool. We know from Chapters 5 and 6 that the destructive and deceptive sides of power can always emerge, and that these elements can entrap an OD consultant.

What are the values that connect or divide those with power? If those with the most power prefer values that champion the status quo, then OD may be seen as a threat. Rather than attack these people directly with a program of radical change, the OD consultant might first approach them on the premise of helping their present organization to operate more effectively. Unfortunately, some OD consultants approach power holders only from the position of their own values favoring human development. Yet if the power holders' values favor cost efficiency, a rationale must be found to fuse human development with cost reduction, perhaps by reducing turnover or absenteeism through job redesign and team building.

Finally, try to identify critical ongoing management activities, such as strategic planning or product development, which garner greater attention from the power holders. Every organization has its own hot spots that attract power, whether it be capital budgeting, promotion decisions, or who sits on what committee. These are arenas in which OD will receive its greatest test and hearing. Keep in mind, though, that you may be dealing with a high slack organization in which work-related activities receive less attention than the political games surrounding self-oriented behavior.

Data-Gathering Methods

We come now to the *how* of gathering data about power. Knowing where and what to look for in searching out power must be accomplished through the skillful application of a variety of methods for gathering data.

The three most common methods for uncovering power are interviews, observations, and routine information already available through company records. Each source yields valuable data about power bases and strategies in use, and these can be cross-checked to determine the validity of any single source. Questionnaires are rarely useful, because greater time and cost are involved in administering them.

Power is a sensitive issue not easily discussed or readily revealed by employees. It would be extremely naive for the novice consultant to walk into an executive's office and ask, "How much power do you have?" Furthermore, the task of the consultant, as understood by the client, is not to engage in a research study on power. You have been hired to address a task-related problem, such as reducing employee turnover. Therefore, if you ask directly about power, the client may think you are deviating from the task at hand.

Stages in Data Gathering

The complex task of data gathering is made somewhat easier because not all of the seven power relationships and various dimensions of power have to be assessed at once. Certain kinds of data become more relevant as the various stages of OD—entry, design, and implementation—progress.

In the beginning, the consultant should focus on data that reveal his or her own power in relation to the sponsor, and the sponsor's power in relation to other key executives in the organization. Without a clear notion of these two relationships, there may be no opportunity to proceed further.

Once the consultant has access to key decision makers, new data are required to understand power relationships between the consultant and each executive, between the executives themselves, and between these executives and decision makers above them. These three assessments permit an understanding of how likely the top group is to support your future efforts.

As the project enters the design and implementation stages, it is important to focus on data about the vertical power relationship between the top decision makers and the rest of the organization, as well as the horizontal relationship between various subunits. Here you begin to know more about who and what carries clout beyond the top management.

Interviews

Our first and most direct interview about power usually occurs with the sponsor, who has the greatest investment in the success of your plan. Still, such information will not likely be revealed voluntarily. You must ask for it. A useful starting point is to inquire about the backgrounds of each of the senior executives. Then, move to a discussion about how these key decision makers relate to each other, and how the sponsor sees his or her relationship with them. Later, ask very directly, "Who tends to side with whom in difficult decisions?" "Who seems to have the most influence in the group?" And, finally, "How do each of these various people view having us here to work on this project?"

Subsequent interviews with key executives become more indirect but still useful. After asking about their jobs and responsibilities, raise questions that probe how the top group goes about goal setting and decision making. "Do they meet frequently?" "What do they tend to discuss?" "Are major decisions made in these meetings or do they get made some other way?" "How was the decision made to invite us in as consultants?"

At times, if the conversation is going well, ask for an example of a recent decision reached over a lot of disagreement. "How did it get resolved?" "Who supported the decision and who opposed it?" Another approach is to ask how the interviewee goes about getting a problem addressed and solved. "How much leeway do you feel you have in making decisions?" "Who will you touch bases with informally if you are unsure about how to proceed?" "Whose support is essential if you want to get results?"

Interviews with lower level managers provide insight into power distribution, as well as a view back at the top. Much depends here on encountering an open informant. Ask, "Which departments here seem to carry the most weight in getting their way about money and promotions?" "Are there any departments that seem to be on the 'outs' around here?" "Can you tell me how the planning process *really* works in terms of setting goals and allocating budget?" "How easy is it to gain access to the top management?" "Do you follow channels, or can you go around them?" And, "How do you see top management here—do they work fairly well together as a group? Who seems to have the CEO's ear?"

Observations

The observation of actual behavior going on around the consultant provides useful notes for checking on the accuracy of interview data. What people tell you in interviews may or may not be found in reality. For example, if the CEO claims an open door policy, yet no one passes through it, what does this say about the CEO's power and his use of it? Consultants often forget to observe the little things, and instead treat the social setting as background noise to the more substantive topic under discussion.

The first clues to look for are in the sponsor's *actual* behavior toward the consultant. Does the sponsor talk *and* act enthusiastically about beginning the engagement? Does the sponsor call you or do you call him? Does the sponsor put more emphasis on discussing next steps than on asking for the consultant's credentials? How does the sponsor react to the consultant's initial suggestions—are they seriously listened to or modified significantly?

With regard to the sponsor's power in the client organization, watch carefully for the length of time it takes the sponsor to gain cooperation from other key executives. Are appointments set up quickly or does the consultant have to remind the sponsor? Must the consultant run a long gauntlet of interviews, just to test his or her credibility. When the consultant arrives for interviews, is he or she greeted warmly and given sufficient time for discussion? Do the executives clearly understand why the consultant is there? And finally, the bottom line, is the budget approved without long delay and nit-picking?

Observations about behavior in the top management group lend insight into their power relationships. Do they react comfortably around each other or are they tense and cold with each other? Do they criticize each other in interviews, or speak with mutual respect? Do they grow quiet and defer to the boss when he comes into the room, or do they treat her as a peer? We often ask to sit in on one of their meetings, keeping an eye out for who does the talking and whose suggestions are accepted.

Power relationships within the organization as a whole are more difficult to observe precisely because of size and scope. Sometimes, a department's physical proximity to the executive suite is an indicator of its rank. Other times, it is the quality of physical decor, the ratio of secretaries to managers, or other signs of resource accumulation. In one all-male organization, we noticed a rigid pecking order denoted by dress differences, with coats and ties for key managers, shirts and ties without coats for managers who were the doers, and shirts without ties for the underlings, and that is how they treated each other. Some of our most telling insights have occurred when we have accompanied a senior executive to the field. Are they treated with excessive deference or friendly banter?

Routine Data

Frequently overlooked is the rich source of data already available in office files. These data are there for the asking, and they can provide a shortcut to long hours of interviews and observations. One hour spent looking for patterns and clues in paper documents can provide several leads to follow up in interviews.

One obvious source of data is the organizational chart, since it shows the design of *position* power. However, it should be supplemented by previous charts to detect who may be moving up or down and which departments have been combined or eliminated. Titles should be studied, because they may differ even when shown on the same level, such as a senior vice president coupled with four vice presidents.

Another important source of data is the structure of committees. Who is on them, who is their chairperson, and to whom do they report? The most salient committees, in our experience, are ones responsible for capital budgeting, strategic planning, and compensation. Once we found the same four people on all three committees, despite other executives listed at the same level on the organization chart.

Other documents to look for concern descriptions of the planning process—is it restricted to top managers or is it delegated to lower levels? And what about the capital expenditure process—are lower level managers given high or low cutoff points for approval?

For each executive, biographical statements may be available about various managers to reveal education and prior experience. Differences in executive compensation can also be important. Even without access to pay records, much can be learned from scanning annual reports and forms filed with the SEC. We once learned from these reports that two members of the top management held controlling stock in the company, although no one had mentioned this fact previously.

And last, an old trick of ours is to enlist the help of secretaries to show us their bosses' calendars. Which subordinates get to spend more time with their bosses? Who goes to lunch with whom? Who attends what meetings? Who cuts around levels to see higher level managers?

Summing Up the Data

We conclude this chapter with a shorthand recording scheme that has proven useful during our consulting engagements (Figure 7–2). It is based on the seven power relationships described earlier and the various power dimensions that need to be assessed. As you read the case of Mega Corporation in Chapter 8, use this chart to diagnose the power and political dynamics in the company. This chart is re-created at the end of Chapter 8 with our initial notes recorded on it. These assessments helped to gauge the types of interventions that were made at Mega.

Mega Corporation
Notes

Power Relationships	*Relative Power* *Hi-Med-Lo*
Consultant to sponsor	
Sponsor to other key executives	
Key executives to each other	
Consultant to key executives	
Top executives to higher authority	
Key executives to organization	
Organization units to each other	

Dimensions of Power
Individual power bases   *Notes*

Department power bases

Predominant power strategies

Distribution of power
  in the organization

Values that divide
  and connect power

Management activities
  that attract power

Figure 7–2
Record of Power Diagnosis

8

Mega Corporation
*Stage I: Consolidating Power
to Prepare for Change*

The previous chapter on diagnosing power began a transition from knowledge about power to the direct application of power in the practice of OD. We continue this direction in the remaining chapters as we consider the Mega Corporation, a real case in which OD and power combine to produce a major organizational and strategic change.

Many of the concepts about power discussed previously are limited to practical applications made by managers on a day-to-day basis. They now assume new meaning and require additional reformulation when extended to the complex dynamics of strategic and organizational change. As a result, we shall introduce a new framework of planned stages of strategic and organization transformation for understanding better how power, when combined with OD, can become a dynamic and unifying force for propelling the process of changing an entire company.

The literature on power stresses the importance of compromise among key power holders in showing why and how organizations gradually change over time. It is decision making at the top that draws their attention, although it is a struggle over resources that is more the focal issue than planned strategic change. When strategic change has been the subject of analysis, the process is typically viewed as a prolonged effort of bargaining and infighting among senior executives over whose vision should win out. This effort gradually emerges into a new pattern of corporate behavior (Quinn, 1980). Pettigrew (1986) describes the strategic change process as

> a political learning process, a long-term conditioning and influence process designed to establish the dominating legitimacy of a different pattern of relation between strategic content, context, and process.

The OD literature has been deficient in proposing new theories of change, preferring to concentrate on methodologies leading to the development of an idealized organization (Friedlander and Brown, 1974). Any blockage of these methods is considered a socio-psychological problem on the part of employees within the organization, to be overcome by a therapeutic program of reeducation, prescribed by trainers and consultants with behavioral science expertise. One lasting model of change used by OD is the general Lewinian three-stage model of "unfreezing, changing, and refreezing." However, it provides little assistance in specifying the critical variables in a particular type of change, such as the relationship between power and strategic change.

A theoretical reconciliation seems in order between political gradualism and OD idealism. We acknowledge that political compromise may indeed explain the typical process surrounding the implementation of major change in most organizations. However, to resign ourselves to a political model seems risky at best and suicidal at worst when we are faced with today's turbulent world of takeovers, global competition, and technical obsolescence. Companies can perish before key power holders respond with concerted action. On the other hand, any OD response to these external challenges that preaches participative management or initiates a quality of working life program seems hopelessly naive and doomed to failure. What is needed is a theory of deliberate strategic change in which an accelerated process is used to facilitate political agreement and unified action.

A close examination of the case of the Mega Corporation reveals a beginning theoretical model for laying out the OD process of how issues of power are resolved in formulating and implementing strategic change. It is a four stage model, and each stage builds upon the other to result in organizational transformation:

Phase I: Consolidating Power to Prepare for Change

Phase II: Focusing power on Strategic Consensus

Phase III: Aligning Power with Structure and People

Phase IV: Releasing Power through Leadership and Collaboration

This chapter describes Phase I in the change process at Mega—Consolidating Power to Prepare for Change. It involves the arrival of a new CEO and his successful efforts to consolidate his power before launching a major change effort. He is later assisted by an OD consultant, and together they plan the first of a series of OD interventions to alter the long-term direction of the company. Chapters 9, 10, and 11 describe each of the subsequent stages in the change process at Mega. In the end, three of the most cherished possessions of any management's power structure—strategy, structure, and key personnel assignments—are significantly altered. Because these three areas are frequently manipulated by top management to maintain their power, they are often ruled out of bounds for OD. However, at Mega, OD becomes a vital process for assisting its power structure to let go of the past and agree on a new future direction.

A great deal of detail is provided in Chapters 8, 9, 10, and 11 about the four phases of change at Mega. Our purpose in doing so is to give the OD consultant a richer appreciation for the intersection between the dynamics of power and the techniques of OD. We will show not only that OD must learn to live realistically with power but that OD can intertwine with power to produce an even greater impact. OD is used by the power structure at Mega to change itself to the point where the organization is transformed in both its internal practices and its external alignment with the marketplace.

The Mega Situation

Tom Rice, President and CEO of Mega Corporation for the past six months, reflected on his concerns as he began planning for the upcoming 1985 fiscal year.[1] In this short six-month period, Rice, an outsider to the propane industry, had learned a new business and taken several actions that had produced immediate improvement in the company's profitability. In spite of these short-term achievements, Rice was concerned about the company's future. The propane industry was a mature industry and Mega was primarily a single business company. He did not see a long-term future for the company, only a short-term focus of meeting cash flow targets set by Mega's holding company, Alpha Industries, which had a large debt acquired in a leveraged buy out (LBO) two years earlier.

Mega's revenues exceeded $500 million and the company was the fifth largest marketer of liquefied petroleum, commonly called propane, in the U.S. Headquartered in Denver, Mega employed 2,500 people and served over 300,000 domestic, industrial, agricultural, and motor fuel customers nationwide through a network of wholesale and retail outlets. These outlets were fed by a distribution system that utilized pipelines, rail tank cars, a fleet of trucks, and strategically located rail and truck terminals.

Late in 1982, Bob May, chairman of Alpha Industries, which had over $1.5 billion in revenues and was listed on the New York Stock Exchange, had decided to take the company private through a leveraged buy out. Alpha's stock was undervalued at nearly 50 percent of book value, and May was worried about being taken over by another company. Bob May, in commenting on the implications of the LBO for Mega, made the following observation.

> The LBO flipped Alpha from having $300 million in equity and $100 million in debt to just the reverse. It made us private and more in control, but the cost of the increased debt to buy it back was $45 million each year in interest. I was unhappy with the performance of Mega and its ability to contribute to paying off the debt, so I brought in Tom Rice to be CEO of Mega.

---

[1]The Mega case is disguised and excerpted from a more extensive research case written by Assistant Professor Arvind Bhambri of the Graduate School of Business Administration, University of Southern California.

The decision by Bob May to bring in Tom Rice as CEO of Mega was a difficult one but one that he hoped would produce a turnaround in earnings at Mega. May had hired Rice the previous year as a management consultant to assist him in restructuring Alpha into three separate businesses, one of which was Mega. At the same time, and unrelated to Rice's consulting project, May terminated the CEO of Mega and assigned one of his corporate vice presidents to be the interim president until a permanent CEO could be selected. May made this comment on his selection of Tom Rice:

> I think everybody was shocked by my bringing in a consultant and putting him in a line role but I think it's something that Tom wanted to do very much and my feeling was that he had a lot of ability, so why not turn him loose on it.

Tom Rice was an ex–Air Force pilot with a B.A. in English and an M.B.A. from the University of Southern California. His initial job had been in real estate finance for a large bank, but he soon left that job to join a management consulting firm in Chicago. Over the next seven years he moved to two other management consulting firms where he became a partner and senior officer, finally heading the regional office of a major international consulting firm. In taking the job at Mega, Rice said:

> Even though I had some qualms about moving to Denver, I took it because I wanted a shot at running a major company. Also, I respected Bob May, and I had some respect from him coming in the door. I didn't see the Mega job as an end in itself. Once it was up and running, I could move on to something bigger. Bob gave me lots of incentive through ownership interest. It gave me a stake in the company.

The Arrival of Tom Rice

Tom Rice took over Mega as CEO on his thirty-eighth birthday. The outgoing CEO called together all of Mega's senior vice presidents for a meeting to introduce Rice. However, Rice was shocked to learn that no advance notice had been given of his arrival and appointment as CEO.

> We were about to go into the meeting together when I asked the former CEO if he had told them about my appointment and he said, "No." So I suggested that maybe he ought to go in and have a few minutes alone with the people to give them a chance to adjust to the news. He went in and, in essence, he said, "I'm going to stay at Alpha headquarters and Tom Rice is going to be the new President. I'll bring him in" And I went in. They were all sitting there demoralized as hell. Nobody had told them why inside candidates had not been considered.

At the meeting, Rice made a few brief comments about how he looked forward to working with the group. He recalled, "It was very uncomfortable . . . they just stared at me." Following the meeting, the former CEO called Rice to tell him that he had planned to fire one of Mega's senior executives because he did not want "to leave Rice with a cancer in the organization." Rice, however, put his foot down and made what he called his first policy decision.

> I decided I wasn't going to change the organization at all— not with the way I was introduced. I didn't trust the judgment of the former CEO. I decided to keep all the people, give them incentives, go through the planning process, and if it didn't work, then clean house. I didn't want to take the risk of starting out fresh and making wrong decisions.

During his first few weeks on the job, Tom Rice concentrated on learning as much as possible about the company and its products. He found the company to be organized into four major functional areas (see Fig. 8–1). The marketing group was by far the largest, composed of over 80 percent of all employees; it was responsible for selling and distributing propane through all of Mega's wholesale and retail outlets. The supply department, with about fifty employees, purchased propane on the open market, and upon delivery turned it over to the transportation department, with about 250 employees, which moved propane by rail and trucks to the outlets. The fourth functional area was administration, with two hundred employees, which included account-

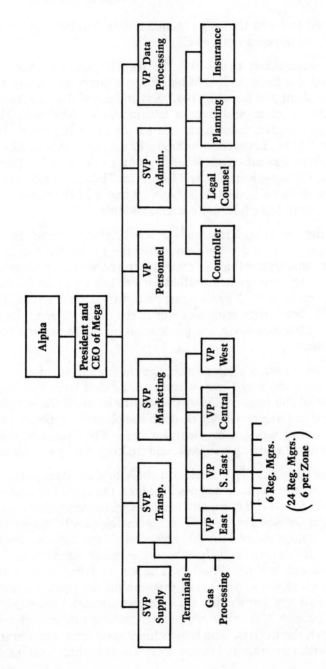

Figure 8-1
Organizational Chart

ing, planning, legal, and insurance. In addition, two small staff groups, data processing and personnel, and the legal counsel reported directly to the president.

Each of the four major functional departments was headed by a senior vice president, and the two staff groups by vice presidents. All of them, along with the legal counsel, were members of the executive committee, which met monthly with the CEO to discuss operating results.

Listed below are the backgrounds of each individual in Mega's top management group.

Name	Title	Age	Education	Seniority
Tom Rice	Pres. & CEO	38	M.B.A.	New
Pat Cook	SVP of Supply	37	B.S.	5 yrs.
John March	SVP of Transp.	43	M.B.A.	7 yrs.
Andy Davis	SVP of Mktg.	40	M.B.A.	5 yrs.
Bill Hope	SVP of Admin.	39	M.B.A.	10 yrs.
Sam Smith	VP of Personnel	44	B.A.	20 yrs.
Ron Mix	VP of Data Pro.	41	B.S.	3 yrs.
Jerry James	Legal Counsel	38	L.L.B.	10 yrs.

Tom Rice was initially impressed with the backgrounds of these seven executives.

They were all relatively young, in their late thirties and early forties, and three of the SVPs had M.B.A. degrees. Most of them, with the exception of Sam Smith in personnel, Bill Hope in administration, and Jerry Cook in legal, had worked for several other companies and had been at Mega for only three to seven years. I felt like I could work with them.

At the same time, Rice was disturbed by low morale among these executives and their subordinates, which he traced to pressure caused by deregulation in the propane industry. The price of propane had been controlled until 1983, and competition was virtually nonexistent. The industry was characterized by a few dominant companies and many small family-owned firms in local markets. One of Rice's senior vice presidents described conditions in the company prior to deregulation.

Up to deregulation, you didn't have to be very smart about how to run a propane company and make money. We still don't have many professional managers. Most people grew up in the company. There has been a lot of nepotism — everyone takes care of everyone else. The people in the field know all the customers by name. You come to work, do your job, take long coffee breaks, and go home at 5:00 P.M., especially here in the corporate office. It still goes on.

After deregulation, increased competitive pressures led to a downturn in Mega's profits. Larger companies in the industry acquired smaller companies, while the overall market demand for propane remained relatively stable. In addition, Alpha demanded a higher cash flow from Mega to meet its debt burden. According to the vice president of personnel, these changes had created low morale among Mega's management:

We've gotten a new CEO every year and there is a lot of uncertainty among the management. Teamwork has disappeared and people are defending their own turf. The philosophy has become "department over company" and "Peter robs Paul to pay Mary."

Actions by Tom Rice

Tom Rice spent his first few days becoming acquainted with his senior executives. He interviewed each senior manager on his perception of the company and the state of the industry. He found them friendly and informative, but guarded and deferential. At meetings with the total group they seemed "closed and very sterile—individually, very nice people but horrible as a team." Rice attributed their behavior to the former interim CEO.

He was very rigorous analytically but a very difficult guy to deal with because he never responded to things specifically—a sort of zero decision making style. People interpreted it as lack of support; in addition, he talked down to people in a parental sort of way. He is the only person I know who refers to Alpha as "the parent."

Within a few weeks, Rice chose to concentrate on two key activities: to negotiate with Alpha for additional incentive compensation to be paid to Mega's executives if they achieved their current 1984 profit plan and to conduct an intensive planning and budgeting process for 1985. Rice was successful in negotiating an incentive scheme with Bob May, although he recalled this encounter as being different from working with May as consultant:

> He was reluctant to change the old formula, but I said, "Look, we've got a situation here where there is no real reward. We have fallen behind plan now and if I drive these guys like crazy to achieve the plan, and they do it, there'll be nothing in it for them. So if you want me to put every ounce of energy into achieving plan this year, give me some incentive." He agreed, but not enthusiastically.

Rice devoted most of his time and effort to the planning process. In a series of day-long meetings, Rice led the executive committee in discussing how they could achieve the current profit plan and in preparing the 1985 plan. He began the process by telling the group that he wanted them to achieve the current plan and then to set ambitious targets for the upcoming year, which included improved revenues, greater cash contribution to Alpha, and a higher return on investment. Rice proposed a set of targets for 1985, which several members of the group said would be very difficult to meet. He also told them about the new incentive plan that he had negotiated with Alpha for achieving the current plan. Each executive then presented plans and budgets for their respective departments. Rice asked most of the questions of each in turn, while the others listened until it was their turn. In every case, goals were raised for each department, as well as immediate steps decided upon to improve current results. When it was over, Rice felt pleased with the outcome.

> It was an excellent forum that enabled *me* to ask questions and that's why I enjoyed it. Very quickly, I learned a lot about the company. We also came up with a laundry list of key issues that had always been there but never put on the table. Airing them was a major improvement even though we couldn't resolve all of them. What came out of

all this was a commitment to achieve our goal this year and next year—and to hell with whether it was the right level; we would try to achieve it.

One of the key actions taken was to raise market prices immediately to increase revenues and thereby achieve the 1984 plan. Several executives argued against it, but Rice persuaded them it was possible because customers seemed loyal to Mega. His response to them was, "Trust me," an expression that he used often in those months when he encountered skepticism. He warned them, though, that they would lose customers later if they did not provide good service.

Revenues and profits increased dramatically, and Mega achieved its 1984 plan. Rice called a meeting of his senior managers and told them how proud he was of their efforts, and that they would each receive a substantial bonus.

At the beginning of 1985, Rice began a lengthy series of field trips to various regions controlled by the marketing department. Each month, he spent two weeks visiting field managers and accompanying them to see Mega's wholesale and retail outlets. Rice viewed the trips as a way to ask questions, learn about the business, and make personal contact with field managers.

> Everyone had told me to go visit the stores when I arrived. But I chose to wait until we achieved the plan and gave out the incentives. I didn't want to visit the field and be on the defensive. Now I had something to talk about. We had achieved something, and we could build on it.

Entry of the Consultant

In December, 1984, Tom Rice called his long-time friend and former M.B.A. professor, Mark Drake, to ask for consulting assistance. Although Rice was pleased with the performance of his senior executives to date, he still had many questions about how he could pull them together for the long term.

> I had very little prior training in long-term planning. I had viewed consulting as a catalyst for short-term change and

I loved the role. All of that is great when you're trying to stir the pot and make something happen, but as Mega develops a higher level of performance, I will either have to shift my thinking about my role or move on to something else.

Tom Rice had known Mark Drake professionally and socially for ten years following graduation from Midwest State. Drake had assisted Rice and a colleague in opening the Chicago office of a Boston-based management consulting firm, and they had worked together on several consulting engagements. Rice later left this firm to become head of an office for another major management consulting firm.

Over the telephone, Rice described his initial experiences at Mega and the actions he had taken: "All I have done so far is to concentrate on short-term results; now I am concerned about the direction Mega will take in the future. We have no long-term plan, and while my executives seem to be concerned about it, they don't know how to discuss or work on it. We still don't have a real team at the top, and I am doing all of the talking." Rice asked Drake to visit Mega's headquarters for a couple days to talk further with Rice and interview his senior executives.

The consultant was received courteously by the seven senior executives reporting to Rice. Two hours were allotted to each interview, and Drake explained to them that the interviews were confidential, no one would be identified by name, and that only general impressions would be reported to the CEO. The guiding questions for the interviews were: Can you tell me more about your job and department? How does your department work with other departments here to get the job done? How do you see the propane industry and its future? How has the company been managed in the past? What is your judgment of the company right now—its performance, strengths, and problems? What actions would you like to see taken? What is your impression of how well the top group works together to solve problems? How do you feel about the new CEO?

Mark Drake was impressed with how open and friendly each of the executives seemed during the interviews. Many of them had prepared notes ahead of time, and Drake took lots of notes. Listed below are excerpts from the different interviews:

Pat Cook, SVP of Supply:
"Tom Rice needs to share his beliefs more with us."
"This company is sleepy and needs more accountability."
"We each stay in our own corners because we've been pitted against each other in the past."
"We are short on gray matter in the middle ranks."

John March, SVP of Transportation:
"We guard our territories too much here."
"We solve problems by throwing people at them."
"Tom Rice shouldn't get too involved in the details."
"Marketing has too full a plate."

Andy Davis, SVP of Marketing:
"Tom Rice is helping things to settle down."
"We have lots of potential in a dead industry."
"We should diversify into more exciting products."
"Our group needs to give more leadership to the company."

Bill Hope, SVP of Administration:
"Tom is slowly bringing us together."
"We aren't clear where the company is going."
"Alpha just wants cash from us."
"Supply and transportation need to be merged."

Sam Smith, VP of Personnel:
"We do very little training in the company."
"Our top guys don't get out to the field enough."
"We wonder if Tom Rice will stay with us."
"There isn't much trust between departments."

Ron Mix, VP of Data Processing:
"We are centralized without giving support to the field."
"We're not unified about how to fit the pieces together."
"Our strategy hasn't been articulated."
"The level of field talent is lacking in marketing."

Jerry James, Legal Counsel:
"Rice has created a positive atmosphere."
"About all we can do here is generate cash for Alpha."
"Marketing is out of control."
"Our market share is going down."

Consultant's Report

Following the interviews, the consultant met with Tom Rice for dinner. Mark Drake gave a brief synopsis of the issues. At the end, Rice expressed surprise that his own personal list of issues confronting Mega was not much different from what was reported. He was also puzzled when Drake told him, "You [Rice] say that you want a team, but they say you prefer to deal with them more on a one-to-one basis." Drake concluded by saying, "It looks like there is a good basis for them to work as a team with you in moving forward." Rice thanked Drake and asked him to prepare a written report with recommendations.

The following is that written report in letter form. The reader may wish to reflect on the situation at Mega and think about what he or she would recommend before seeing what Drake recommended.

Dear Tom:

The purpose of this letter is to expand on what I outlined at dinner. The interviewees were very open and constructive in their comments. As we agreed before my arrival, the purpose of the visit would be to get a feel for the company through confidential interviews, and to report the major areas that need further attention from top management. Listed below are the main topical headings and issues that I could decipher.

I. *The Top Group*

How do we structure the group better? Do we need two groups, one composed of Rice and the SVPs to drive strategy, and a larger group to review and set policy? How often should various groups meet, and what should be their charter? How can we improve the way we work together informally? How do we improve the level of trust, and reduce turf protecting? Can we discipline ourselves more in meetings? How can we divide up various corporate tasks and hold people accountable?

II. *Product Flow or Distribution Process*

Should we develop an in-depth study to determine the real costs of moving propane through the system, and the best ways to manage the flow? Can we articulate better how customer problems and inquiries get handled so that our response is better? Should we go to a transfer pricing system from supply to marketing? How can the SVPs of marketing, supply, and transportation work more closely together to improve the efficiency of the process?

III. *Corporate Strategy*

What short-term (1 to 2 years) strategies should we set for ourselves? How do we improve inaccuracies in market forecasting? Should we keep the wholesale business? How do we go about capturing greater market share against sleepy competitors? What should be done about the southeastern region? Should we concentrate our focus on certain market segments? What do we do about terminals and gas processing? What long-term (3 to 5 years) strategies should we adopt? What kind of diversification strategy, if any, should we have? Should we develop a supply business for other LPG firms? What R&D should we undertake? What do we do about Alpha and the LBO?

IV. *Organization Structure*

Do we have the right balance in our structure? Is marketing too large as a single organization (80% of our employees)? Should we divide marketing into two departments, east and west? Should transportation be folded into supply? Do we have too many levels in marketing? Should data processing and personnel report to the CEO? Should training and safety continue to report to legal? What should be our overall position on centralization versus decentralization?

V. *Corporate Staff*

Do we have too many people in some staff groups, especially accounting and data processing? How do we improve the response of data processing to our information needs?

What do we do about the general staff attitude, which seems to be slow and still attuned to the regulation days? Do we have enough high-powered talent below the top level? Do we need a few sharp analysts working directly for Rice and the top group? Do we have enough people in legal to handle lobbying? Are we short on safety people?

VI. *Personal and Team Development*
Tom Rice seems to be well received; he wants us to achieve together. He needs to reflect a positive image to the employees and to the industry. He can be more direct in sharing his beliefs and opinions with us. We are not sure if he really wants to solve problems in a team. We need to do more cross-training and job rotation. How do we learn to solve conflicts better without making them a threat or a personal issue?

The above are the main questions evoked during the interviews. There is a lot of agreement for many of the issues, though a lot of differences in proposed solutions. Everyone expressed a strong desire to work together with you.

My suggestion is that we design a retreat for all of us to meet together to discuss these topics, flesh them out some more, and develop whatever action plans that are needed. If you decide to hold a retreat, we will need to design a format to approach the various issues in the most constructive manner. It may be that some issues deserve more focused discussion, while others can be tabled for another meeting.

You may want to pass a copy of this letter on to the others so that they know what I reported to you. It could also serve as a basis for planning a future meeting.

I look forward to seeing you again in the near future. Please give my thanks to the others for their warm reception.

Sincerely,

Mark Drake

Power and OD Analysis

This chapter reveals how Tom Rice laid a foundation from which he could begin to lead a major change effort at Mega. Through a series of critical actions over six months, Rice consolidated enough power to influence his key executives into taking the next step of reexamining the strategy of the company in its marketplace.

As can be seen from the consultant's notes in Figure 8–2, Rice began with a substantial power base of position, expertise, and political access in relation to Alpha's chairman. However, he could not immediately begin a large-scale change project. He faced a group of disgruntled and disappointed executives who had been passed over for the third time in three years. Their power bases were also substantial—ones of information, tradition, and expertise in the propane industry. Given their serious doubts about whether a former consultant could learn their business, they might easily decide to wait out Rice as they had done with the previous CEO.

Yet there was an opening for Rice if he carefully adapted his power strategies to the political situation. Mega's senior executives were not really united as a coalition to oppose Rice. Power was fragmented and diffuse among them, and they did not have great power over the rest of the organization. Under pressure from Alpha and each succeeding CEO, these senior executives had retreated into their departments, each engaging in turf-protecting political behavior. Only the marketing SVP, Andy Davis, had substantial departmental power based on its centrality and lack of substitutability, controlling over 80 percent of the company's employees. But Davis personally lacked a necessary individual power base of tradition in commanding his field organization, because he was younger than his peers, highly educated, less experienced, and relatively new to the company.

The company was also vulnerable to change, because it was in a state of confusion and low morale, and caught in the transition from a high slack to a low slack system. Previously, it operated in an industry whose prices were regulated, an economic atmosphere that allowed the company to make money in spite of its quality of management. Even after deregulation, Mega's

Mega Corporation
Notes

Power Relationships		*Relative Power* *Hi-Med-Lo*
Consultant to sponsor	– CEO former MBA student of consultant – Asked by CEO to work on previous consulting projects. – Counseled CEO on career – No authority over CEO	Med to Hi
Sponsor to other key executives	– CEO picked by Alpha Chairman over inside candidates – CEO former consultant to Alpha Chrm. – CEO new to job and doesn't know propane business.	Med to Hi
Key executives to each other	– Marketing is strongest with so many employees. – Others have some dept. base – Most have MBAS/prof. mgmt. background	Hi Med
Consultant to key executives	– Represents the CEO – Academic/MBA professor – Older experienced consultant – Outsider – doesn't know business – Has no authority over them.	Med.
Top executives to higher authority	– CEO picked by Alpha Chrm. but has to prove self under LBO. → Med. to Hi – Other top executives not selected to be CEO. → Lo	
Key executives to organization	– Several are new to organization. – None picked to be CEO – Several are MBA's without long experience in propane – In culture that values experience and tradition	Med to Lo
Organization units to each other	– Marketing controls 80% of people – Admin. controls information – Supply purchases propane – Transportation delivers Rivalry	Highest Standoff – each has base

Figure 8–2

(continued)

Dimensions of Power	*Notes*
Individual power bases	−CEO has Knowledge−mgmt. consulting−also Political Access to Alpha Chrm. −Other top mgmt low in industry Experience−mainly have dept. bases. −But all top mgrs, including CEO, lack Tradition and experience in the company.
Department power bases	−Marketing highest with most employees − Others have different bases − each with some Centrality (Supply & Transp.) −Admin. has information control
Predominant power strategies	− Lots of turf protecting between depts. − Don't work together. − Dept. Heads waiting out CEO? − No obvious Coalitions or alliances
Distribution of power in the organization	− Field managers have power through autonomy, distance, & experience in propane. − Formal authority centralized at top with professional managers. − Budget is downward.
Values that divide and connect power	− Each SVP & VP operates separately − Field organization values tradition and experience − Pay attention to dept., not company
Management activities that attract power	− Exec Committee is main decision making formal group. − Previous decisions made 1 to 1 with CEO − Budgeting is key activity.

Figure 8–2, continued
Record of Power Diagnosis

culture was still attached to self-oriented behavior; many managers were not changing even though there was market pressure for change.

Rice's power strategy was to start from his prior base of expertise in management consulting. He did not try to compete with his managers' knowledge of the propane industry or tradition of experience in the company. Instead, he established a new set of rules geared to work-related behavior. He treated his senior executives as a problem-solving team, not as separate, disparate individuals. He focused on needs of the target group, asking them lots of questions and showing respect for their damaged egos, a behavior to which they were unaccustomed. He worked around roadblocks by negotiating with a key decision maker, Alpha's chairman, for increased rewards in return for short-term performance—a bargaining action intended to encourage work-related behavior in a high slack system. He also proposed unconventional solutions (e.g., raising prices), and, when members of the team expressed reservations, he was persistent saying, "Trust me."

Fortunately, Tom Rice's power strategies and decisions proved correct; positive results were immediately forthcoming in the forms of short-term financial performance and higher compensation. With a reputational power base established through the success of his initial actions, Rice then chose to visit employees in the field, where there would now be fewer challenges to his lack of knowledge about the industry.

The net result was that Tom Rice had consolidated his power to the point at which his subordinates were increasingly dependent upon him for leadership. This stronger power base enabled Rice to begin planning for a large-scale change in the company's strategy and its structure. It also allowed him to invite an OD consultant to intervene. Mark Drake acted similarly to Rice by asking questions, valuing individual points of view, and discussing his role in an open manner. They responded in like form, not only because of the consultant's demeanor but because of his political access to Rice.

The consultant's report did not recommend a threatening change in the way Rice and his group had been proceeding. In proposing an off-site retreat, he sought to continue a process of team problem solving that Rice had started.

The phrasing of the report, by playing it straight in raising rather than answering questions that were stated in familiar business terms, demonstrated the consultant's beginning expertise and information power base without usurping power from the other executives.

The next chapter describes how Rice and the consultant built on these changing power dynamics to focus the group on steps that would resolve their disagreements about long-term business issues.

9

Mega Corporation

Stage II: Focusing Power on Strategic Consensus

OD rarely is involved with senior executives as they make strategic decisions about the future direction of their companies. One explanation is that the power structure at the top reserves the so-called "big issues" as its exclusive domain. Another, more telling reason is that OD has likely failed to offer a convincing rationale and workable process for becoming directly involved in strategic planning.

Instead, OD has largely confined itself (and been confined by top management) to activities geared to making the present organization work better. Changes are limited to internal subunits, focusing on improving leadership styles, building teamwork, and resolving intergroup conflict. OD rationalizes its contribution to the future state of the organization by assuming that long-term success can be assured through effective practice of the collegial/consensus model at lower levels of management in the "here and now" organization.

In this chapter, we contend that OD can (and should) make a valuable contribution to the strategy formulation and implementation process. In fact, we argue that it is essential because traditional planning methods used by senior management have often failed in their intended effect. After examining why strategic planning and OD must become more interdependent, we return to the Mega case to see how this can be done.

Failure of Traditional Strategic Planning

Recent years have witnessed the demise of strategic planning departments in many companies. Elaborate formal plans developed by staff analysts and submitted to line executives have seldom been implemented. To replace this expertise, top managements have turned to outside management consultants. But again, the results have been disappointing. Lengthy reports with detailed recommendations have often gone unheeded by managers, who seem more concerned with the current bottom line than the uncertainty of future results.

Research to explain the failure of traditional strategic planning methods has recently been forthcoming from scholars of politics and culture in organizations (Mintzberg, 1978; Quinn, 1980). They set out to study the planning process as it *actually* occurs in corporations. From their findings it is possible to infer an informal strategy making process that undermines and overcomes formal plans developed by top management and consultants (Greiner, 1983):

- Strategy evolves from inside the organization, not from its outside environment.
- Strategy is a deeply ingrained and continuing pattern of management behavior that gives direction to the organization — not an easily manipulable and controllable mechanism that can be easily changed from one year to the next.
- Strategy is a nonrational concept stemming from the informal values, traditions, and norms of behavior held by the firm's managers and employees — not a rational, formal, logical, conscious, and predetermined thought process engaged in only by top executives.
- Strategy therefore emerges out of the cumulative effects of many informal and formal actions taken and decisions made daily over many years by many employees on all

levels — not a one-shot event engaged in annually only by top management.

These skeptical political scholars argue that the traditional approach fails because it does not adequately take into account the political realities and pluralistic nature of modern organizations. Self-interest prevails over corporate goals. Vested interest groups protect their existence. Cultural traditions prevent an honest look at environmental realities.

However, if their assumptions are valid, we are left with a paralyzing dilemma. The market environment of a company can change, even rapidly, as in the case of the shift from audiotapes to compact discs, but top management can do little to change itself, except through a gradual and lengthy process rooted in political compromise and cultural inertia. Hence, the death of companies occurs over time.

An OD Rejoiner

One answer to the political determinists has come recently from the "new leader" school of management (Bennis and Nanus, 1985). Their contention is that organizations can be moved in new directions by a powerful CEO with a vision — who, through his or her personal behavior, models new values implicit in the vision. These values, because of the positive way in which they are communicated through face-to-face contact, inspire people to embrace not only the new values but the vision itself. The old values are shed and a new culture emerges. Hence, the organization is transformed.

Our position is that the "new leader" school offers only a beginning rationale for motivating people in organizations to change their behavior toward a new strategic direction. Although there is considerable evidence from social learning theory to suggest that modeling behavior by authority figures can alter employee behavior, charismatic leaders are few and far between, and opportunities for extensive personal communication are limited in all but the smallest organizations. Moreover, this approach underestimates the power of environmental and political realities raised by the determinists. Visions are naturally limited by external economic conditions and internal resources, and many employees are understandably reluctant to commit their own careers to a visionary leader who offers nothing more than a dream.

What has been missing in simplistic approaches to planning and leadership is an OD process for intensively focusing the power structure on gaining consensus and commitment to a particular strategic direction. In the absence of such a process, "politics as usual" takes over as private disagreements about strategic direction prevail. We conceive of this OD process as a necessary base in a triangle that causes one side, the power elite of the corporation, to clarify and reach in-depth agreement about the other side, the strategic business issues affecting the long-term direction of the organization. (See Figure 9–1.)

It is here in the Mega case that OD demonstrates that it can provide a unifying process for assisting a fragmented and resistant power structure to come together in making realistic strategic decisions that are, in fact, implemented.

Retreat Design

The first Mega retreat was designed by the CEO, Tom Rice, and the consultant, Mark Drake. Holding a retreat was only one

Figure 9–1
OD as a Foundation for Strategic Change

of several alternatives; Rice could have met alone at the office with his executives and addressed various issues and made decisions about each one; or he could have decided alone what to do; or he could have called in a management consulting firm to make detailed recommendations. Instead, a retreat was chosen because it seemed to build upon the following assumptions about the existing political situation at Mega:

1. The top group seemed ready to follow Rice's leadership and it was concerned about many of the same issues that he was. They had already begun talking about them and there was conviction that the issues were important. Rice wanted to keep the momentum going that had produced such positive short-term results.

2. Rice wanted the group to feel more involved and powerful, believing that on his own he could not make the necessary changes, and even if he tried there would not be sufficient commitment from his subordinates to carry out his decisions.

3. The business issues facing them were many and varied, yet they seemed interrelated. It was hoped that further discussion in a reflective setting would add greater clarity to the issues. In addition, the retreat would serve to flush out individual differences of opinion that could be confronted and hopefully resolved.

4. Rice and the consultant believed that the group was competent and in possession of much of the necessary knowledge about the company, its products, and the industry in general, and therefore it could develop realistic and workable solutions by sharing this knowledge with each other.

It was decided to organize the agenda for the retreat around three broad topics: strategy for the company, organization structure, and the team at the top. There was no clear consensus about the future direction of the company, and there were many questions about the adequacy of an organization structure that had not been changed in years. An underlying issue to both subjects was the need for greater teamwork and less turf protecting among the key executives.

Finally, Rice wanted the consultant to lead the meeting so that he could become part of the group. He told the consultant:

> The group is looking to me too much, and I don't have all the answers. They have to become more active and vocal with their points of view. Maybe they will do that with you leading the meeting.

Another reason for the consultant to lead was so that he might act occasionally as an educator who, through short lectures, could provide new ideas and frameworks on certain subjects for enlightening the discussion.

As it turned out, these ambitions proved only partly realizable in one retreat. Nevertheless, substantial progress was made toward reaching an agreement on a new strategy.

The First Retreat

The retreat was held in a no-frills hotel about thirty miles from the corporate headquarters. Rice did not want a lot of distractions. The conference room was composed of a large U-shaped table with chairs, several flip chart easels, and a coffee pot. All eight members of Mega's executive committee attended, beginning on Friday noon and finishing Sunday noon. The consultant invited an assistant, Jim Ware, who was especially knowledgeable about strategic planning.

Tom Rice began the meeting by stating what he hoped to achieve:

> I want us to keep going from the good base we have laid so far. You guys have been great in coming through with short-term results. Now we all know that it will take more than that — we have to look farther ahead. I'm not sure where we should go, but I think this process may help us to discover it. I've got no hidden agenda. I just want us to dive in and see where it takes us. My role will be to join in with you, so I have asked Mark Drake to lead the meeting.

Mark Drake handed out the agenda (See Appendix A) and asked the group if it made sense to them as a starting place, adding that they could modify it as they proceeded. They all agreed; Andy Davis, SVP of marketing, said, "If we can accomplish all this, we are certainly off and running."

It is impossible in this short book to give a detailed account of what transpired. Therefore, we will highlight the most significant events and accomplishments.

The initial discussion on strategic issues turned out to be much longer than the time alloted for it on the schedule. Jim Ware began by presenting a strategic framework to analyze their situation (Porter, 1980); it centered on making an assessment of the propane market to predict future opportunities and threats. Several flip charts had been filled when an important interchange took place between Rice and the group:

Rice: Why do you guys see so many threats and so few opportunities?

March (SVP of transportation): Because the market is so mature and customers for LPG are limited.

Cook (SVP of supply): Besides, even if we could sell more propane, we don't have any money for reinvestment because all our cash has to go to Alpha to pay off its debt.

A long discussion followed; Rice argued, "I feel that we can take control of our own destiny, no matter what the external environment says. Don't let's blame others for why we can't take control." The group listened intently but was not convinced. Several argued for diversification into other markets, but also wondered where they would get the capital.

To explore these issues further, the consultant divided them into two subgroups, and told both to go off to another room for two hours to identify two to four strategic alternatives that Mega could follow, and list the pros and cons of each alternative.

When the subgroups reported back, there was much more support for Rice's earlier plea. Diversification was still a distinct possibility, but there seemed to be more enthusiasm for concentrating on the propane market. One group, in which Rice had been a member, contended that the propane market still had many opportunities and that the competition was "sleepy." A compromise was argued by Andy Davis who said, "The company

can stay with propane but sell other products to present customers, such as insect control for the home." The consultant in-
terrupted to ask the group to think about various alternatives
overnight, and that they would come back to them the next day.

After dinner the first evening, the group met to discuss its
members' leadership styles and ways of working together as a
team. The consultant introduced this more traditional OD exercise as a potential means for achieving greater understanding and
emotional solidarity among the diverse personalities in the group.
Up to this point, their interpersonal relationships had not been a
legitimately discussable topic, just as strategic planning had not
been. The consultant assumed that continued progress on the
business issues would be limited unless the group also was able
to address more openly their working relationships.

Each member of the group was asked to fill out a leadership
style questionnaire on both themselves and each other (based on
the *Managerial Grid*, 1964). In addition, they completed a blank
at the bottom of the page asking for a "strength" and an "area for
improvement" for each person. These results were then circulated to everyone and a discussion ensued with each person allocated twenty minutes to discuss his feedback with the group.

Good humoredly, the group completed the paperwork.
During the feedback session, their comments were quite gentle
and understanding. Each person controlled his time and asked
how he might improve. Tom Rice was characterized as a "9–1"
directive leader, which seemed both to please and concern him.
He explained to them, " I know you see me as very demanding
but I want to work together as a team." The group told him that
they wanted more meetings to address problems instead of talking on a one-to-one basis, and he agreed.

The second day explored the topic of organization structure. Again, a short lecture on different structural forms was followed by subgroup meetings to propose various alternatives for
Mega. Their presentations resulted in a heated discussion where
some members expressed a preference to keep the current functional structure while others argued for breaking up the marketing organization into east and west groups, and still others
thought they should shift to a product structure with the wholesale business separated from the retail business.

The subgroups' lack of consensus on organization structure prompted the consultant to return the group's attention to
the question of strategy. Mark Drake and Jim Ware both discussed how a clearer strategy might help them to decide on an
appropriate organization structure. Drake presented the idea of
developing a written strategic statement with the following characteristics:

- sums up the company identity and direction
- is a written document prepared by the key executives
- is brief and clear in its words
- is exciting for them to pursue
- can be communicated and understood by all employees

In addition, Jim Ware provided the group with a set of potential topics they might wish to address in their statements:

- Service/Product Description — What do you provide to
  the marketplace?
- Target Market — Who is your primary customer?
- Delivery Method — How do you approach the customer?
- Financial Goals/Standards — What results do you hope
  to achieve?
- Management Practices — How do you expect employees
  to go about making decisions?
- Stakeholder Treatment — What do you give back and
  what do you expect from vested interest groups?

The group agreed that preparing a statement would be
valuable, so the schedule was rearranged to permit more time on
this assignment. Subgroups again met to draft a statement. Each
presentation from the two subgroups was greeted by spontaneous applause. Although there were superficial differences, both
groups had proposed strategies that concentrated exclusively on
the propane industry, emphasized a strong marketing approach,
set high financial goals, and used acquisitions as a means for
growth.

The most lengthy and energetic discussion occurred
around financial goals because both groups had surprised themselves by setting very high growth targets. They wondered if the
goals were realistic, and after suggesting ways to increase market

share and make acquisitions, the group unanimously agreed to set a goal to double revenues and profits in five years. The afternoon meeting ended in an atmosphere of great excitement.

After dinner on the second evening, the group decided to meet socially and play "Trivial Pursuit." The vice president of human resources, Sam Smith, had brought the game with him. Immediately, the staff executives teamed up to play against the line managers (which included Rice, Cook, Davis and March). It was a close game with much banter and humor. The line executives won on the last move, and gloated over the staff with such comments as "Thank god, the line has some brains in this group." The staff managers vowed, "We'll get even next time," and they all resolved to play again.

The last morning was devoted to action planning for the next steps. The group agreed that the vice president of administration, Bill Hope, would prepare a working draft statement of the strategy, to circulate it among the others for comment, and then to hold two or three meetings with middle managers to solicit their reactions to the statement. In addition, they agreed to gather quantitative data on various questions raised that would either support or refute the group's desire to concentrate on the propane market.

Tom Rice closed the meeting by saying:

> I feel we have made great progress in this meeting. We came up with a lot of good ideas, but, more important, we have started to come together about what we want to do. The strategic statement can provide us with a guidepost for sorting out many of the issues still facing us, so let's get that statement as soon as possible.

Following the meeting, Tom Rice met with the two consultants to review the meeting. Rice was quite pleased with the results, and said, "We argued about a lot of tough questions and no one got bent out of shape. The group really pitched in and I hope we can keep this spirit going." They agreed that Jim Ware should write up the detailed notes he had kept during the meeting, and that these notes should be circulated to all participants. Mark Drake suggested they talk about follow-up actions to the strategic statement. Rice replied, "We need to hold a second retreat to re-veiw and ratify the final strategic statement, and then we can go on to discuss our organization structure."

Power and OD Analysis

The design of the first retreat reveals both Rice's and the consultant's recognition of the Political/Pluralistic model of orga-nizations. They started at the top of Mega with its most senior managers and their diverse views of where the organization should be headed in the future. Rice had entered Mega when its management was in a *schizoid* state — it was trying to cope with market uncertainty brought on by deregulation. Due to leader-ship problems created by the previous authoritarian CEO, Mega's senior managers had retreated to protecting their individual and departmental turfs. Rice stepped into this negative situation by creating several short-term successes, yet this was only a tempo-rary solution that did not resolve the long-term identity of the corporation. Hence, the need to focus on strategy and structure for the entire company was made clear.

Other consultants with Collegial/Consensus or Rational/ Bureaucratic models in mind might have proceeded quite differ-ently from Mark Drake. The traditional OD consultant, wedded to the Collegial/Consensus model, would likely have focused solely on interpersonal relationships and team building. A Ra-tional/Bureaucratic consultant would probably have prescribed a lengthy analytic study and set of detailed recommendations for Rice alone to implement. Mark Drake combined aspects of both these models by using a group process to focus the political actors on analyzing business issues.

The retreat design was also congruent with the power styles of Tom Rice and the consultant. They relied on their bases of expertise, reputation, and professional credibility in pursuing *playing it straight* power strategies by using data to convince oth-ers, focusing on needs of the target group, and being persistent. Interestingly, Rice relaxed his earlier dominance somewhat by passing the role of moderator to the consultant and becoming part of the group. We can surmise that he was trying to shift the direction of his influence from downward to sideways power in building a stronger alliance across his entire top team.

At the start of the meeting, members of the group felt powerless in being able to redirect the company and improve its performance over the long term. However, Rice intervened in his charismatic, "trust me" power style to express his belief that they could, in fact, take more control over their own destiny. They subsequently found it difficult to talk about organization structure without first resolving questions of strategy. Rice did not force them to talk about strategy, nor did he advocate one point of view; they discovered for themselves that strategy was the essential point to resolve. Then, as they explored various strategic alternatives, they began to coalesce around one direction for the company.

Much of the prior rivalry in the group began to dissipate as they found strong areas of agreement. By using subgroups, the consultants moved them toward consensus. Instead of hearing eight separate opinions, they melded their ideas into two reports that revealed considerable overlap. Andy Davis, with a strong departmental power base in marketing, had ceased to argue so strongly for diversification. His self-oriented behavior had been neutralized by the work-related commitment of all his colleagues to narrow the strategic focus of the company.

The group also found that they could talk openly about many issues, even about personal styles with Tom Rice present, and without hurting one another or feeling a loss of power. Their defenses were slowly being lowered. These accomplishments, and their new-found team spirit, were celebrated with social play in the evening. Interestingly, instead of competing as individuals, they chose to compete in organizational terms — line versus staff. The winning coalition of line managers would become prophetic as they were to become more dominant in subsequent meetings. The perceived need for a written strategic statement became the main "pulling" product of the retreat. It focused attention and energy, and it gave the group not only a sense of accomplishment but an involving task to continue their efforts. By the end of the meeting, various individuals took responsibility for follow-up efforts in preparing a draft statement.

Rice and the consultant were concerned whether this momentum would continue at a second retreat. The consultant told Rice:

> If the group can agree on a strategic statement, it can help to depersonalize the structural and personnel decisions. A statement to which they are intellectually and emotionally committed can be held up against any self-oriented suggestions about position power in the organization. We can ask, "Do their suggestions fit the new strategy?"

Looking back on this retreat, we can see how an OD process, with its particular techniques, was used to advance the top management of Mega into a second stage of change, *focusing power on strategic consensus*. Complete agreement on a new strategy, however, had not yet been reached, perhaps for individual reasons centered on concerns for what a new strategy would mean for their power positions. The next chapter shows the completion of the second stage and a launching of the third stage of structural and personnel changes.

Appendix A
Tentative Agenda for Mega Retreat

Friday, February 8

12:00–1:00   Lunch

1:00–4:00   *Strategic Issues and Opportunities*
              We will try to identify the short-term and long-term
              strategic issues and opportunities facing Mega. In par-
              ticular, we want to get a clearer focus and specify the
              alternatives, along with their pros and cons.

4:00–5:30   *Overall Corporate Organization Structure*
              We will analyze the present structure and its strengths
              and weaknesses. How well does the current structure
              fit the current strategy? Then, before adjourning, we
              will begin a discussion on what types of structure best
              fit with the strategic alternatives identified in the
              prior session.

6:00–7:30   Dinner

7:30–9:30   *Team Building Session*
              We will use some self-evaluation techniques to take a
              closer look at the functioning of the group, and talk
              about plans for building an even more effective team.

Saturday, February 9

8:00–10:00   *Overall Corporate Structure (cont.)*
              We will continue from yesterday by examining the re-
              lationship between different structures and the strate-
              gies identified yesterday.

10:00–12:30   *Distribution Flow*
              We will discuss the present situation and how it can
              be made more effective, ranging from how to price it,
              how to measure it, and how to make it more respon-
              sive to the customer.

12:00–1:30   Lunch

2:00–5:00   *Corporate Staff Organization*
              This discussion will focus on the structure of the staff
              in Denver and the climate in the office. We will look

at how it can be made more effective, ranging from who reports to whom to norms for performance.

5:30–   Dinner

Sunday, February 10

9:00–10:30   *Committee Organization at the Top*
               Discussion of what is the best way for the top executives to organize themselves. What kinds of committees do we need, who should be on them, and what should be their charter?

10:30–12:00   *Action Planning*
               We will review and summarize the specific plans that we made during the meeting. Who will do what to follow up?

Note: This outline is tentative and flexible, depending on progress we make and preferences of the group.

10

Mega Corporation
Stage III: Aligning Power with Structure and People

Many corporate strategies are never realized, even after top management groups participate actively in formulating them. Key executives make a commitment to pursue a new strategy, only to return to business as usual. The principal reason for non-implementation is the refusal of top managers to adjust their jobs and roles to make them more consistent with the new strategy. They resist change in organizational structure because they fear a loss of power. Hence, no exemplary model or incentive for change is provided to lower level managers.

This chapter examines the third stage of organization transformation — how OD can assist top management in restructuring itself in translating strategy into action. We begin by considering various schools of thought about organization design, and then we see how Mega's senior management built upon these schools to create a new structure in which all senior executives, except for the CEO, changed jobs and roles.

Organization Design

Three important schools of organization design bear on how OD, when combined with power, can contribute to the restructuring of organizations. Deficiencies in these schools create an opening for the introduction of OD — how OD can and should play a vital role in redesigning the jobs of political actors.

One approach is called the *task design* school (Galbraith, 1973). Its credo is to design the structure to fit task requirements so that people can focus better on the work that has to be performed. Because tasks vary in difficulty from being relatively simple to highly complex, the organization structure must also vary to facilitate the completion of these tasks. Numerous research studies have demonstrated, for example, that mechanistic structures facilitate the accomplishment of relatively simple tasks, while organic structures are more appropriate to complex tasks (Burns and Stalker, 1961). Position power becomes more concentrated at the top of a mechanistic structure, while it is distributed widely in an organic design.

A weakness in the task design school is made evident by the political school (Pfeffer, 1978). These scholars contend that organization structure is the product of self-interest, and is formed through negotiation and compromise. At the top of the organization is the dominant coalition, which takes care of its own interests in formulating the stated goals of the organization. Rational prescriptions, the kind advocated by the task design school, enter in only as one of many factors to be considered in designing a structure that is acceptable to the dominant coalition.

An exclusive focus on either the task design or political school is likely to produce dysfunctional consequences for strategic and structural change. To design a structure that only matches the interests of the powerful few may advance the status quo more than the future strategy of the company. Or to create a rational design that goes against vested interests will likely not be implemented.

A third school, *self-designing organizations*, stresses the behavioral process through which structures are created. It has gained prominence in the design of innovative manufacturing plants (Mohrman and Cummings, 1987). This school argues that employees should be included in designing the work system that affects them. Otherwise, people will not be committed to a new system, regardless of its technological sophistication.

The self-designing organizations school takes us a step

closer to how OD may contribute to structural redesign at the top of organizations. It incorporates rational task design into a participative process that draws on the ideas and interests of those directly affected by the design. However, there are limitations in directly extrapolating this approach to top management, because its experiments have largely been confined to factory level jobs. The political issues are different at the factory level, where lower level workers are seeking to acquire power instead of fearing the loss of power. Furthermore, jobs at the factory level tend to be more concrete and easier to specify than for senior management.

At Mega, we see how a unique OD process, drawing upon the strengths of all three schools, was created to deal with the dilemma between self-interest and rational organizational design at the top management level. In the second and third retreats, Mega's senior executives completed work on a new strategy and then used it in redesigning the structure and their positions within it.

Second Retreat

Tom Rice, CEO of Mega, arranged for the second retreat to be held seven weeks later at the same hotel. In planning the retreat, Rice and the consultant, Mark Drake, assumed that one and a half days would be sufficient to decide upon a strategy and organization structure. Once again, they underestimated the amount of time required for achieving consensus.

As a first step in the second retreat, Rice and Drake chose to place initial emphasis on reaching agreement about a written strategy statement (Appendix B contains the retreat agenda). Their hope was that the statement could be used as the principal criterion for selecting an appropriate organization structure. They were reluctant to begin the structural discussion until a clear strategy had been decided upon with the full agreement of the group; otherwise, the discussion might be dominated by concerns of self-interest. Drake recommended that the strategy be written in precise and concrete words in order to clarify differences of opinion and to avoid loose interpretations that could be self-serving.

A single draft statement was presented to the group by Bill Hope, SVP of administration (Appendix C). He had prepared it after receiving several recommendations following the first retreat, including a ten page statement from Andy Davis, SVP of marketing, who began his contribution with this preamble:

> I believe my ideas and intuititions are very much on track and were confirmed at our first retreat. I am optimistic, therefore, that they can serve as the basis for an effective Mega long-term strategy. We must strike soon and become the market leader or some other company will seize the position. Once lost, that position will be almost impossible to achieve.

In addition, Hope had interviewed all members of the group, except Tom Rice, who said, "I'd rather wait and hear what the group prefers."

The draft statement presented by Bill Hope was greeted by several comments expressing strong approval. At this point, Mark Drake asked them to split into two subgroups so they could closely examine the draft statement and ask the following questions:

- Is it enduring but also selective enough to aid in screening major decisions?
- Does it address all major stake holders?
- Does it express the long-term standards and values to which the organization aspires, instead of short-term targets?
- Is it brief enough, yet does it consider:
  major markets?
  attitude toward risk?
  differences from competition?
  desired management philosophy?

Both subgroups reported general agreement with the statement, although each group asked that it be refined to state explicitly that the company would focus exclusively on the LPG industry, and that Mega would be selective in choosing geographical markets that looked most promising. They also wanted a reference to the need for the acquisition of other LPG firms to increase market growth.

Jim Ware then asked the group to test the statement and it refinements against some recent decisions that they had considered. One such decision was a potential acquisition that had been rejected. The group concluded that the strategic statement would have ruled out the acquisition because the acquiree had "questionable values" for treating customers. Another rejected decision, one that proposed entrance to a new market area, was also matched against the statement, and the group concluded that they had been wrong in originally rejecting the decision. Pat Cook, SVP of supply, exclaimed, "I wish we had this statement then, and we'd be farther along today."

Tom Rice concluded the discussion on strategy. He asked Bill Hope to draft a final version that could be tested one more time back in the company. Jim Ware then led the group in a discussion about what additional quantitative data were needed about the industry to assure that the statement was viable. They also developed a plan to expose the statement through discussions with three or four groups of middle level managers at Mega.

At this point, just before dinner, the group appeared ready to move on to a discussion of organization structure. However, before doing so, Tom Rice summed up the afternoon by saying:

> Let me state what I think we have decided, just to be sure that I understand and that everyone is on board. We have committed ourselves to concentrate on selected market segments within the propane industry, increase our marketing emphasis, raise the level of customer service, set high financial goals, and make acquisitions.

The group returned after dinner to begin a discussion of organization structure. The consultants presented two alternatives, based on discussions at the last retreat. One alternative was to retain but refine the current functional structure; the other was to divide the company into a product organization in which one group concentrated on retail markets and the other on wholesale markets. Another structural issue centered around the corporate staff; whether to put it all under one person or to form two groups, one directed toward external affairs (e.g., finance, public relations) and the other toward internal affairs (e.g., personnel, data processing).

Mark Drake gave a brief lecture on key issues to consider in its deliberations on structural design:

- The *horizontal* issue: What should be the major groupings: functions or product areas?
- The *vertical* issue: How should authority be allocated: decentralized or centralized?
- The *integration* issue: How and where does the organization come together: at what level and through what committees?
- The *fit* issue: All choices should be made against their fit with corporate strategy, not with personal preference because people come and go in companies.

Again, two subgroups were formed to meet and discuss the pros and cons of the various structural alternatives. They were asked to report back in the morning.

The next morning both subgroup reports generally argued for retaining the present functional structure because there was insufficient growth in the wholesale market to warrant a product structure. One group proposed the addition of a major new marketing function, designed to promote product development and new sales programs for the field organization. However, this was opposed by Andy Davis, SVP of marketing, who contended that he could do the same thing within his present field organization. As for the corporate staff, the debate was quite heated and unclear. The VP of personnel, Sam Smith, felt that he should continue to report directly to Tom Rice, as did the VP of data processing and the legal counsel.

In essence, everyone argued for retaining their present power base, which the consultant pointed out to them. They responded with laughter. Mark Drake suggested that the group was not keeping in mind the implications of the new strategy; for example, should a separate function be created to deal only with acquisitions? John March said, "It doesn't look like we're going to a product structure, but we've got to go back to the drawing board in figuring out the best functional structure." They agreed to meet for a third retreat.

The meeting ended on a mixed note; the group felt excited about the new strategic statement but frustrated with their lack of progress on organization structure. Nevertheless, Tom Rice complimented the group on their progress, and then said, "Let's all think some more about organization structure before we meet again at the next retreat."

Third Retreat

Prior to the third retreat, Tom Rice met with the two consultants to plan the agenda. Rice began the meeting by saying:

> We need to move these meetings off the discussion level and into action. I'm ready to move and the group seems ready too. But they seem to be waiting for me to make a decision, and I will do it. All of our checks on the strategy statement made sense, and I am comfortable with it. So now the question centers on organization structure and who fills what jobs? This is going to be tough.

Four hours later they had developed a plan and agenda. Rice would lead off the meeting with his interpretation of the strategy and his view of the required organization structure to match the strategy. Then the group would discuss the advantages and disadvantages of Rice's proposal. Once a structure was settled upon, they could then discuss the responsibilities of each key job. Finally, they would try to select the people who were qualified for each job.

In mapping out a proposed structure (see Figure 10–1), Rice and the consultants decided on a new functional structure that made five significant changes.

- Form a new marketing group that would be separate from but develop programs for the field organization, which would be renamed the operations group.
- Form a new corporate development group that would be responsible for acquisitions and finance.

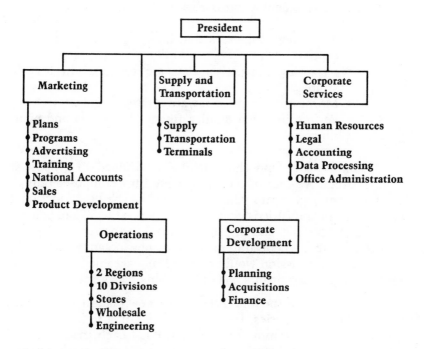

Figure 10–1
Proposed Organization Chart

- Combine all remaining staff functions under a new corporate services group.
- Combine supply and transportation together under one group with the same name.
- Flattens the field organization so there would be fewer managers and more direct reports to each manager.

For each of the major functional groups under a senior vice president, they drew up a proposed description of its key charter; an example for the new corporate development group is outlined below:

To pursue aggressively the acquisition of propane companies and to redeploy current assets through:

- Acquiring businesses that have high added value potential.
- Divesting businesses that are marginal in Mega's
  strategy.
- Monitoring progress toward strategic goals.
- Performing high quality financial analysis and planning.

Finally, Rice and the consultants decided to propose a
smaller executive committee reporting to him, composed only of
the four senior vice presidents from each of the new functional
groups. As a result, Rice decided not to invite the VPs of personnel, data processing, and the legal counsel to the retreat. He felt
that they were not central in making the new organization work,
and that the discussion would be more manageable with five instead of eight participants. He outlined his reasoning:

> I need to sell the four SVPs on the new plan first and focus
> on their anxieties. I know they are going to be very con-
> cerned, some more than others. But I can't manage more
> than four of them, and they are key. If I can sell these four,
> then I can sell the others. Also, I can't give personal over-
> sight to all those staff functions. They should be staff to
> the organization, not to the CEO. Our field stores have
> been complaining about the lack of responsiveness from
> the staff. It needs direction from someone other than me.

Before the retreat, Rice sat down with the three noninvi-
tees to explain his reasons and to seek their suggestions on issues
that should be discussed at the retreat. They expressed strong disappointment at not being included but offered numerous suggestions for Rice to consider. He promised them that he would discuss with them any conclusions reached at the retreat
immediately upon his return.

The third retreat was set to last for two days, beginning
after lunch on June 28 and continuing through the morning of
June 30 (see Appendix D for the agenda). It was held in Colorado

Springs at an expensive and comfortable resort hotel. Each of the participants received a packet of materials beforehand, including an abbreviated statement of the strategy developed at the second retreat (Appendix E) and a letter outlining Rice's objectives for the retreat (Appendix F). In addition, the consultants prepared a series of flip charts for Rice to use in presenting his recommendations.

Tom Rice opened the retreat by stating to the group that he was ready to make major decisions, but hopefully only after the group had reached a consensus about them. He stood up and made a formal presentation with the flip charts. He started with the redrafted and abbreviated strategy statement prepared after the second retreat, and a list of its pros and cons.

Pros	Cons
• Clear, focused goal to channel employees' energy.	• Increases stake in a mature industry.
• High profit strategy in fragmented industry.	• Delays transition to a diversified company.
• Alpha more likely to understand and support.	• Senior executives may not find it challenging enough.
• Able to be implemented with current management expertise.	
• Facilitates eventual transition to a diversified company if that becomes necessary.	

Rice stated that he was very excited about this strategy and would commit himself to it, yet he wanted to be sure that the others felt the same. Everyone responded with enthusiastic approval, and they asked him to continue.

Next, Rice described his proposed organization structure. He went through the chart and described what he called the "charters" for each major functional group. He ended with the pros and cons, as he saw them, of the proposed structure.

Pros	Cons
• Simplified structure grouped into key functions.	• Change from current structure.
• Fits strategy of focused growth in propane.	• Adjustment time of individuals.
• Uses existing talents as a springboard.	
• Facilitates development of clear performance charters.	
• Brings CEO closer to key functions.	

Rice said, in his closing comments, "OK, I've talked a long time and told you where I stand. Now I would like you to feel free to shoot holes in it." Mark Drake then asked the group, "Well, what do you think?"

They nodded approval, then asked Rice for clarification of certain details. The conversation became more animated when Andy Davis, SVP of the current marketing group, said, "I'm worried about this new marketing group being separated from my operations group." Rice said, "First, can we talk about the structure without putting names in the boxes? I really tried to design it to fit with the strategy, and that is the key issue, not who goes where. My reason for separating marketing from the group is because we said that we have to build a strong marketing emphasis and I'm worried that it will get submerged if left as a small function inside operations." Davis retorted by saying, "Yeah, I understand, but there is going to have to be a lot of coordination between the two groups." Rice agreed, and said, "That will be up to you guys. I don't want to be the arbiter."

As the afternoon progressed, few serious objections resulted, and enthusiasm seemed to build for the merits of Rice's proposal. Members of the group added advantages that Rice had not thought about; they found that the new jobs seemed to be more challenging than their present jobs. One disadvantage emerged when Pat Cook asked, "What is going to happen to some of our regional and zone managers, because we have eliminated some of those jobs by going to only two zones and fewer regions?" Before Rice could reply, John March said, "It will give us an opportunity to remove some deadwood that we should have cleared away before now." Rice nodded his head as March was speaking.

Mark Drake closed the afternoon meeting by asking, "Am I right that you, as a group, feel reasonably comfortable with this proposed structure and are ready to move on to talk about people?" They agreed, and Andy Davis quipped, "Now it's going to get interesting!" Everyone laughed, and Bill Hope half-jokingly challenged Tom Rice, saying, "Is your job up for grabs too?" Rice smilingly said, "If you can make a case for it. Let's go have dinner and relax a bit."

The next morning began with a lot of energy from the group as they addressed Mark Drake's assignment question: "Before we talk about people for various boxes, can we go through each key job and discuss its skill requirements? We need to understand better the attributes that each incumbent should have." The entire morning was devoted to this assignment, and the group responded with numerous ideas about skill and experience requirements.

After lunch, the group nervously waited for Drake to describe how they would approach the selection of people for the key jobs. During lunch, Drake and Rice had agreed to a plan in which each person, excluding Rice, would write down on a piece of paper their answers to three questions:

1. Who in this room, or outside it, do you think is best qualified for heading each function?
2. Which job is your first choice, and which is your second choice?
3. Which job is your last choice?

Upon receiving the assignment, the group appeared somewhat surprised. Bill Hope asked, "Do we have to sign them?" Tom Rice told them, "We have to talk about this openly, which has been our way of doing it all along, but we have to do it systematically, so let's begin with a ballot to see where you stand on all the jobs." It took only a few minutes for them to write their choices. Everyone signed their ballots and handed them to Drake and Ware who posted the results on the blackboard.

All the participants stood up to watch the tabulation. To their amazement the first choice of each individual also matched the majority choice of the group, except in one troubling instance.

New Function	Self First Choice[1]	Majority Choice
Corporate Development	Bill Hope	Bill Hope
Operations	John March	John March
	Andy Davis	
Marketing	No one	Andy Davis
Supply and Transportation	Pat Cook	Pat Cook
Corporate Services	No one	Outsider?

[1]Their current jobs were: Hope, SVP, of administration, March, SVP of transportation, Davis, SVP of marketing, and Cook, SVP of supply.

The principal dilemma in the balloting centered around Andy Davis; he wanted to keep his present job in charge of the field organization, which was to be renamed from marketing to operations. However, the group preferred that Davis switch to the new marketing function. The group tried to reassure Davis that they thought his talents were most needed in the marketing area, which was to receive added emphasis in the company. Davis admitted that it was his second choice, but he felt that he was the only one in the group who really knew the field managers.

Rather than pressure Davis for a decision, John March turned the discussion to the new corporate services job that no one wanted and where everyone preferred someone from outside the group. They discussed the other three vice presidents who had not been invited to the retreat, and a strong consensus emerged for Jerry James, the legal counsel. They felt that he was a strong manager and that was what the staff area needed. Rice joined in this discussion to say that he agreed with their comments about James.

The group seemed reluctant to return to the question of

Andy Davis, who had reacted with obvious disappointment over the group's preference for John March in his current job. At this point, Mark Drake turned to Tom Rice and said, "Perhaps we should take a break here and think about it before dinner, if that makes sense to you?" Rice responded, "Look, I feel very good about the way we have handled this. We seem to know where our basic talents match up. It's been a long day, so why don't we go off and relax a bit, and then we can return to our discussion after dinner."

When everyone had left the room, Tom Rice said to Mark Drake, "I'm going to see Andy Davis and persuade him to take the marketing job. You order a nice dinner for us here in the meeting room, and get a couple of bottles of champagne. We're going to celebrate!"

Here is Tom Rice's account of his meeting with Andy Davis:

> I found him and we went off to sit outside on the resort's grounds. I had decided beforehand that he should take the marketing job, and I was prepared to lose him if he decided to leave the company. But I didn't think he would. He liked marketing issues too much and was spending most of his current job on them. I sat down with him to listen, but not to give him a choice. First, I explained what I saw as his strengths, and those are what I needed in the marketing job. I made it very personal. I told him that I wanted him to be part of the new company, and that he would make a big contribution to it. I said that I would do anything he wanted to make the job work. I also said that I truly wanted the team to stay together. Andy knew it was a heartfelt sentiment and he knew the rest of the team felt the same way. We talked for two hours about all the things he could do in marketing, and in the end he agreed. He's a very emotional guy.

Three hours later the group returned for dinner. They were greeted by a waiter pouring champagne. Andy Davis smiled and told people that he was going to take the marketing job. Tom Rice offered a toast: "We have made some very big decisions over the last two days and I am proud of this group. We have set ourselves a strategy that all of us believe in, chosen an organization that will make it happen, and each of you has a new job where I think you can be very effective. Let's toast our goal of doubling this company over the next five years and all of us having a lot of fun in doing it." The dinner followed, with the group in high spirits.

The next morning was devoted entirely to action planning. They agreed that no one should say anything back in the company until Tom Rice had spoken to the Alpha chairman to receive his approval for their decisions. They helped Rice to strategize for this meeting because it would mean that Alpha would have to regard Mega as more than a "cash cow" to pay off Alpha's debt. In addition, assuming that Alpha approved, they planned a meeting for later in the week to select people for the field organization, as well as for the other jobs that would be created. One of these openings was the legal counsel's job, and the group's preference was to appoint the current assistant legal counsel, Alice Short, to the job. Rice acted pleased with that suggestion, and said, "She will be the first female officer in the company."

Power and OD Analysis

In this chapter we have seen the top management of Mega — its dominant coalition — coming together in an open forum where they not only defined a new strategic purpose but came to grips with their own personal power and roles in implementing that strategy. OD played a vital role in facilitating these major decisions over a short time in a spirit of open debate among the key power holders. At the same time, the OD process cannot be fully understood without placing it within Mega's political context.

Critical in the second retreat was securing consensus and commitment from the top group to a new strategy that they felt could guide their future actions. As mentioned previously, the organization had been in a schizoid state in trying to cope with uncertainty in the marketplace. The new strategy, supplemented by Rice when he filled the power vacuum as CEO, provided a clearer and more focused sense of corporate identity to replace defensive political behavior centered around departments. Most important to this process was the fact that the strategy was developed largely by the group and without active intervention by Tom Rice.

The new strategy provided a strong benchmark for then judging the adequacy of structural alternatives. Still, when it came to deciding on a specific structure, members of the top group retreated quickly into their self-interests. They preferred to keep the current organization and their positions in it. At this point, the CEO exercised his power to prescribe a structure that, in his opinion, best fit the new strategy.

The effective use of power by Tom Rice broke the resistance of the group in altering the structure. Rice stepped in to give direction when the group could not bring itself to act. After doing so, he withdrew to encourage the group to discuss and criticize his presentation. They could not undermine it because Rice had closely aligned its logic with the new strategy that the group itself had created and accepted.

We see here how Rice used his initial power bases of *expertise* and *information*, in pursuing a *playing it straight* power strategy. In addition, he used his newly formed bases of *reputation*, and even *charisma*, to *work around roadblocks*. Rice employed all of his substantial power bases and their related power strategies to achieve acceptance for his plan.

Interestingly, Rice and the consultant met beforehand and "behind the scenes" to orchestrate the setting and content of Rice's presentation so that self-interests of the participants could be dealt with within the framework of his presentation. Rice invited only the four top officers of the firm to the retreat, thus enabling him to focus exclusively on needs of this target group. Rice's recommended structure was not threatening; it resembled the present functional organization, and it contained more positions than could be filled within the group. Each executive could see opportunities for enhanced positional power for himself within it.

An OD technique was used to facilitate the resolution of the most difficult power issue in organization design — aligning key executives with new positions in the organization structure. Rarely is this sensitive issue handled so openly in most corporations. The traditional method of the CEO selecting executives "behind closed doors" can not only damage the losing egos but diminish commitment to implementation. Instead, Rice permitted open choice, perhaps as a way of rewarding the group for accepting his structural recommendations. The group was then able, with intimate knowledge of each other and from information acquired during the preceding discussion of each job's requirements, to reach rapid consensus on who they thought were the right people for the right jobs — except in one case.

The case of Andy Davis shows how Tom Rice intervened again to use his considerable power to resolve a potentially difficult problem. Davis was reluctant to give up his strong power base. Although Rice was prepared to let Davis go, he decided first to appeal to Andy's strengths in marketing, coupled with an emphasis on serving the greater organizational good. The initial holdout of Davis and his subsequent acquiescence to a personal appeal from the CEO helped him to appear and continue to feel like a powerful member of the team.

The broader implications of these decisions for organizational power and strategy implementation should also be noted. Every key job at the top was changed, with two new functions added to give greater power to marketing and acquisitions. A smaller executive committee was formed that contained only five people who had the most powerful jobs. Three former members no longer reported directly to the CEO. A new dominant coalition had been solidified, one that would likely reach decisions more rapidly. Organizational power had been simultaneously tightened and decentralized. A tighter power structure had been formed at the top to drive the new strategy into reality. The group had so thoroughly discussed the charter of each new function that the CEO would unlikely have to intervene to tell his subordinates what they should be doing. In addition, there were fewer managers assigned to the two top levels in the new operations organization, and more stores would be reporting to fewer and better managers.

At the end of the third retreat, the top group was mobilized and focused, feeling more powerful as a unified team, with a plan of action that would affect many other people. Still, nothing had been implemented beyond the top group. The next chapter examines the results in the fourth phase of change.

Appendix B

Agenda for Second Mega Retreat

9:00–12:00   *Fine-Tuning the Strategy Statement*
Key Questions:
1. What is strong about Bill Hope's statement?
2. What is missing in his statement?
3. Will it give us direction?
4. Will it box us in or liberate us?
5. How can it be communicated effectively?

12:00–1:00   Lunch

1:00–3:00   *Developing a Management Philosophy Statement*
Key Issues:
1. Values about what level decisions should be made.
2. Values about involvement of employees in decision making, planning, and goal setting.
3. Values about performance appraisal.
4. Values about employee development.
5. Values about staff orientation.

3:15–5:30   *Reevaluating Basic Organization Structure*
Last time we had two structures proposed to us. Can we examine them to determine how consistent they are with the strategy statement we have prepared. Which is more consistent? How might we make a transition toward one of these structures? What actions are most feasible now; one year from now; two years from now?

5:30–7:00   Drinks and dinner

7:00–9:30   *Fine-Tuning Present Organization*
Last time we had several suggestions about improvements that could be made within our present organization. What should we do about:
1. *Supply-transportation interface*-should they be combined? How can they work together more effectively?
2. *Marketing organization*-Does it need new functions (e.g., director of domestic sales, director of industrial and national accts.)? Should some functions be divested (e.g., acquisitions, truck fleet, wholesale

sales, etc.)? Should regions be consolidated and better balanced?
3. Do we have some functions in the wrong place? For example, not only some under marketing but safety and training under legal, training scattered around, wholesale pricing in MIS?

Sunday

8:00–11:30   *Improving the Corporate Staff Organization*
Last time we had some alternative models suggested, as well as a philosophy of how staff should relate to the line organization.

Key Questions:
1. Should all staff be consolidated under one SVP of administration?
2. If not, what is the logic for a second set of staff responsibilities, such as one for administration and one for corporate development?
3. What is the position with regard to decentralization? How can that be implemented more effectively?

Appendix C

Draft Strategy Statement

Strategic Statement

Mega is a marketing and distribution company. In defining and managing our businesses, we will strive to achieve the following goals:

Markets
We will actively seek markets in which we can achieve leadership by differentiating ourselves from our competitors. We will accomplish this by adding value through goods and services that we offer to our customers. These goods and services must always meet high standards of excellence that we wish to be associated with our company. These standards include: service; reliability; integrity; and safety.

Organization
We will orient our organization toward the needs of our customers. Our organizational structure, information and administrative systems, communications programs, and compensation/incentive systems should facilitate service to our customers to the greatest possible extent. Generally, a decentralized decision-making process encourages customer orientation, and we will push authority down as close to our customers as possible.

Growth
We do not see growth as an end in itself. However, we believe that growth is a logical and necessary outcome of a well-managed company. We value growth for the characteristics that it fosters—such as innovation, energy, and risk taking—and the high-quality people that it attracts. We will encourage growth both from our existing asset and employee base and from acquisitions, where they fit us organizationally and strategically.

Business Base
We will invest in businesses that give us diversity in our business mix. Such diversities increase our growth potential, reduce our reliance on any single market or business segment, and create new opportunities for management development. In making specific decisions about new business opportunities, we will give the greatest weight to those that build on our existing market and organizational strengths and that offer attractive long-term financial returns.

Perspective
We must constantly maintain a view toward the long term. We will establish long-term objectives; devise systems to measure our performance against them; and make adequate investments to ensure the viability of the company far into the future. When necessary, we will endure short-term problems and dilutions of profitability for the sake of long-term performance.

Employees
We recognize that our employees are the foundation of our company. Consequently, it is our duty to maintain a high-caliber work force. This means that it will be necessary for us to hire high-quality people; compensate them fairly; encourage them to high standards of performance; provide a safe, comfortable and efficient work environment; deal with them consistently and fairly; and invest in them to develop their skills and enhance their careers.

Profits
We have an obligation to our shareholders, our employees, and the communities in which we operate, to generate profits that will nourish the health of the company. We expect financial performance that exceeds industry norms in all our businesses, and we expect to provide our shareholders with an attractive return on their investment in Mega, considering the risks inherent in our business and returns available from alternative investments.

Appendix D

Agenda for Third Retreat

Objectives

1. Reach consensus on a shared vision of what Mega should be in the future.

2. Design organization structure, key roles, and personnel assignments.

3. Make commitment to a specific plan of action to implement vision and organization.

Schedule
Friday, June 28 at 1:00 P.M.
Vision and Organization Discussion:

1. Presentation by Tom Rice

2. Group Discussion

   a. Does the vision make good sense to us?

   b. Does the vision fit our first and second retreats' statements of strategy and values?

   c. Does the organization fit the vision?

Adjournment at 5:00 P.M. Casual dinner at 7:00.

Saturday, June 29 at 8:00 A.M. - Continental Breakfast
Personnel discussion:

1. What are the skill requirements for the key jobs?

2. Who should fill these jobs? What are the individual preferences?

Adjourn for lunch at 12:00.

Saturday, June 29, at 1:00 P.M.
Plan of Action Discussion:

1. How do we develop a plan to "sell" Alpha?

2. What are the specific steps for change?

3. Who will do what and when?

Adjournment at 5:00 P.M. Dinner at 7:00

Sunday, June 30 at 8:00 A.M. Continental Breakfast

Continuation of Plan of Action Discussion

Adjournment at 12:00. Sunday Brunch in the Main Dining Room.

Appendix E
Redrafted and Abbreviated Strategy Statement

Mega is a leading distributor and marketer of LPG and related services.

We set aggressive financial goals and achieve growth through market development and acquisitions.

Our people establish a competitive advantage in selected market segments through a unified effort that demands:

- A strong marketing orientation.
- High standards of safety.
- Outstanding service "before our customers need us."

Appendix F

Letter from Tom Rice on Third Retreat

TO: Senior Vice Presidents
FROM: Tom Rice
RE: Agenda for Third Retreat

This note will give you a briefing on the planned agenda for our Colorado Springs retreat.

My objective is for us to reach consensus on our future strategy, the organization required to get us there, and the roles and positions that key people will fill.

We have done a lot of thinking so far in getting to this point, and now I feel it is time for us to move to a plan of action. We have the opportunity to design an exciting future for the company and ourselves, if we all join together and commit ourselves to making it happen.

To get us headed in that direction, I will start off the discussion at the retreat by laying out my personal vision for the company and my views on the required organization. From there I would like you to join in to discuss my views, search for areas of agreement and disagreement, suggest alternatives, and so forth—but, hopefully, by the end for us to reach agreement for a specific plan of action that we can review with the other officers and begin to implement by November 1.

As some preparation, I would like you to review our prior work (I have enclosed Bill Hope's latest draft of a strategy statement), and do some thinking about your goals for the company and yourselves personally. Come prepared to add creative input. I want us all to openly air our thoughts.

I have asked Mark Drake and Jim Ware to work with us as facilitators. I want them to participate because, though I have some specific ideas to share with you, I also want to hear and discuss your views in an open forum before reaching closure. They have helped me in preparing the agenda for the meeting, as well as sending along the three enclosed articles that they thought may be relevant to our discussions. I have already sent you one article, but I think it is worthy of another look.

I am looking forward to our meeting, and to coming up with a vision that all of us feel will take us in a promising and rewarding direction.

11

Mega Corporation

Stage IV: Releasing Power Through Leadership and Collaboration

A strong foundation had been laid by Mega's top management at the preceding retreats for translating their plans into action. Significant changes had already occurred; the top group had created a new vision for the company and redefined their roles in a new organization structure. Now, in this fourth and final stage of strategic change, they attempt to lead the rest of the organization in joining them to move ahead.

This chapter describes the broader implementation effort and its results at Mega. We then look back to understand better why OD, in combination with power, was able to play an important role in helping to unify and energize Mega's management, and thereby to change the strategic direction of the company. This analysis will also call attention to political conditions in the company that made it susceptible to change; these conditions may vary across organizations.

Changes in the Company

Tom Rice was successful in persuading Alpha's chairman co approve the proposed strategic, structural, and personnel changes developed at the third retreat. In commenting on this meeting, Rice said:

> It went well, not just because the chairman had confidence in me, but because I gave him a plan that made sense. He felt that we really had our act together and that Alpha would benefit from it. I showed him that we could meet Alpha's short-term cash needs and still have additional funds for growth and acquisitions over the long term.

Immediately after Alpha's approval, Rice called a one-day meeting of the new executive committee to plan a public announcement and to arrange for all the rippling effects of additional personnel changes that would occur. Just before this meeting, Rice met with the VP of personnel, VP of data processing, and the legal counsel to explain the results of the third retreat. Although the first two VPs expressed disappointment in not reporting to the CEO and having to report to a new SVP of corporate services, they were enthusiastic about all the other changes. The legal counsel excitedly accepted his appointment to be SVP of corporate services, and Rice told him to meet immediately with the other two VP's in an effort to build a new working relationship.

The executive committee meeting was conducted by Tom Rice with Mark Drake in attendance. Following the third retreat, each senior vice-president had immediately begun to plan for how they wanted to organize their functional groups. Several new jobs were proposed in marketing and corporate development, and the operations organization was to be slimmed down. These plans were reviewed and approved by the executive committee before they began to discuss individual names for various jobs.

Throughout the discussion of personnel changes, Rice kept emphasizing that, "We have to get the right people in the right jobs, meaning those who can really implement our strategy." A list of candidates with high potential was printed on a blackboard. These names were scrutinized for special talents, compatibility with people for whom they would work, and readiness for promotion. In all, thirty-nine executives in the firm changed jobs; two people were dismissed and three were retired early; and three new positions of vice president were created.

Next, the executive committee discussed how they would introduce the changes. Many individuals had to be met with immediately to see if they would accept their new positions. Some individuals were to be offered more than one position, leaving it to them to decide. In addition, a "celebration," as Rice called it, was planned, to which all field managers and the corporate staff would be invited to attend a large meeting set for the following week in Denver. Rice's objective was to use the meeting as a special opportunity to communicate, in a positive way, the new strategic direction to all key employees.

The celebration was held for two hundred employees in a large warehouse on the grounds of the corporate headquarters. It was a festive environment with a band, food, and banners displaying "Double in Five Years" on them. Tom Rice made an emotional speech that began: "Many of you have been wondering if this company has a future, and now I am here to tell you that it does. We are going to double the company in five years and every one of you is needed to make it happen and to benefit from it." He described the new strategy and organization structure, a copy of which was distributed to everyone. Key personnel changes were announced, and several senior vice presidents spoke briefly to the group about their plans.

As a postscript to the celebration, Tom Rice wrote a note to Mark Drake:

> The vision has been communicated! All went well. I feel real enthusiasm and, of course, am now driven to deliver. Last night, driving home after the executive dinner with all the managers, I found myself smiling. I am pleased with our results, and here we go!

During the following year, literally hundreds of decisions were made at many levels in the organization. Several new marketing programs were launched, and a new information system for reporting results more rapidly was implemented. The asset base of the company also changed dramatically; six acquisitions of propane distributors were made and nonpropane facilities were sold.

One last retreat was held during this period to review accomplishments and to make decisions about additional changes. The primary focus was on how to extend the change effort into lower levels of the organization, especially to the retail stores. They decided to eliminate the entire zone level in corporations, moving top management closer to regional and store managers. An intensive training program was planned for store managers, along with a sales incentive program based on company profit sharing.

Another significant decision made at the retreat was to hold a conference in Dallas for the operations organization. All senior managers attended and each regional manager was asked to bring one outstanding store manager. During the meeting, Tom Rice spontaneously took the floor to describe both his vision for the company and the ways he expected employees and customers to be treated. Small groups were used to identify problem areas and to propose solutions, a method that was learned in the prior retreats.

Afterwards, Tom Rice commented:

> This was the first time that a large group like this had been assembled for a meeting, let alone conducted in such an open manner. It gave me a chance to say how I really felt, which avoided the filtering effects of so many levels in the organization. I didn't do it in a planned way; I just stood up and said what I thought and felt.

At the end of one year, Mega's financial performance had improved significantly. The company was several million dollars over its profit plan, and its return on assets had risen 40 percent. The same rate of financial accomplishment continued throughout the second year, and it looked like the company would double itself in three years, two years ahead of schedule. These results led to greatly increased compensation for employees at all levels.

Unleashed Energy

Near the second year of the change effort, Tom Rice made this comment to Mark Drake as he reflected on the results at Mega:

> The most amazing part of this whole thing is how people at all levels responded. The previous CEO thought I should

fire some of my key group, but I wanted to see for myself. They more than rose to the occasion. Then, when several people got new jobs, they really produced! New ideas were coming from everywhere. It was like this monster had been asleep for twenty years and finally woke up.

The motivational impact of the many changes on the wider organization had been underestimated by Rice and his top group. In the early stages of the change process, they had been preoccupied with solving the business issues that they thought would improve the financial performance of the company, and, beneath that, with their own positions in a changing power structure.

But the results of their efforts had given many other employees a clearer direction for their efforts — "focus on propane marketing," and hopeful growth goal of "double in five years" — all of which was communicated with a great deal of fanfare and employee involvement. The top people not only moved into new jobs, but many others also took on new responsibilities. And the revised profit-sharing system permitted significant increases in pay for many employees.

A young manager several levels removed from the senior group commented on the effects of these changes on him personally:

I was very disappointed when I first came here because new ideas were not welcome. I was just about ready to leave when the lights came on. The whole place seemed to do an about-face. I got a new boss who listened to me, and he was giving me more work than I had done in years. I felt like we were going somewhere.

Still another manager at the store level said:

Before Tom Rice, those guys in Denver rarely ever visited my store, and then it was to find something wrong. Now I feel like they are actually trying to help me. My sales have gone up a lot, and my paycheck is a lot fatter too.

And a senior vice president reflected on changes in his style of leadership:

It is so much more fun to be leading instead of trying to cover myself. I found out that Tom Rice trusted me with a lot of latitude in my job. So I got my people together and said "It's a new ball game. Let's get on with it."

The traditional and depressed culture of Mega had been uplifted by the many changes; many employees had identified with the new sense of corporate purpose and its supporting structure within which they saw greater opportunities to take initiative, make decisions, work together, and be rewarded.

Looking Back — Power and OD at Work

Mega was transformed from a sleepy company without hope to a dynamic and growing firm because of many factors. On the surface, the change was aided by a combination of individuals and events: Tom Rice becoming CEO, a consultant entering with a background in OD, a series of retreats to promote reflection, a clear and focused strategic statement, restructuring of the company toward the marketplace, and many people receiving new jobs with greater responsibility.

Interestingly, as we probe beneath these events for underlying forces, we find an absence of many of the popular techniques suggested in the old and current OD literature, such as charismatic leadership, or management by walking around, or team-building exercises, or bottoms-up participation, or intergroup confrontation meetings, or action research, or quality of work life programs, or leadership and interpersonal training for the entire management.

We see quite clearly that the change effort at Mega was planned and directed from the top; first, by the new CEO, Tom Rice, then by Rice and the consultant, and finally by the top team. The process of change evolved, as we have shown in Chapters 8 to 11, through four distinguishable stages with critical issues of power to be resolved for organizational and strategic transformation to take place.

To initiate a break from Mega's past, the chairman of Alpha had to decide to replace the former CEO with Tom Rice, who was excited and enthused by the opportunity. Rice moved rapidly to consolidate his power by using a collaborative but highly directive power style to accomplish short-term results. The group learned quickly, though not necessarily consciously, that they could succeed if they worked together under Tom Rice's leadership. None of these changes were accomplished with the assistance of OD, although a favorable foundation was laid for its subsequent use.

In deciding to call in an OD consultant, Tom Rice said:

> I had no experience in being a CEO. Everyone started looking to me for all the answers. This was hard for me to deal with because I had no game plan; I didn't know the industry and they did. All I knew was the process of management.

Rice's use of the consultant fit well with his power base/ strategy connection, that of using *expertise* from his management consulting background to *focus on needs of the target group*. His technical knowledge of the propane industry was limited. If he had relied on the department heads for this knowledge, he might have lost his leadership hold on them. To prevent this, he shifted the focus to broader management issues — strategies, structure, and personnel. He also added greater weight to his power base by *forming a coalition* with a consultant who was well versed in these same subjects as well as an OD process for addressing them. When the retreats started to become bogged down in difficult areas, Rice intervened with a power base of *charisma* and a power strategy of *being persistent* to get decisions made.

Perhaps surprising to those versed in OD, the overt topics at the retreats were largely business issues, not behavioral relationships. Careful analyses and vigorous debates took place about Mega's marketplace and the resources needed to increase performance. In the end, the top group chose to lead from its traditional strengths by concentrating on an industry they already knew, by fine-tuning the functional organization structure that previously existed, and by tapping the potential of managers who had worked at Mega for years. In essence, they had chosen to renew and refocus their existing resources.

Although it took a single powerful leader to initiate these

efforts, OD provided a collaborative process at the retreats to consolidate political factions at the top around a common goal. Moreover, this process enabled the group to reexamine its members'
own power positions and to make significant changes in their formal positions and roles. Out of these retreats, the top group developed a strong alliance and collective power that led and supported changes throughout the company. Their renewed strength,
energy, and direction were transferred through both a planned and
unplanned process of leadership behavior that involved and empowered other employees. Many new leaders had been spawned.

We can surmise that members of the top team, through an
implicit process of social learning in the retreats and from observ-
ing Tom Rice, had applied this knowledge on the job through
their own behavior. They had learned the value of (1) seeking
open collaboration to address sensitive, work-related issues, and
(2) acting as assertive leaders to bring this collaborative process
to subordinates. One of the SVP's subordinates made this comment on his boss's behavior after the retreats:

> It was like night and day. My boss used to be very distant
> and hard to read. He made all the big decisions, often with-
> out talking to us. But later he brought us together and
> seemed to delight in our wrestling with problems that I
> didn't even know we had.

At the same time, one of the SVPs, Andy Davis, who had
resisted the creation of a new marketing department, maintained
a degree of subtle competitive rivalry with the new head of the
operations department. Although Davis worked hard to create
new marketing programs within his newly formed department
and to give strong support to the company's strategy, he left it to
his successor, John March, to initiate collaboration with him.
Tom Rice and OD had succeeded in getting Davis to take on the
new job but not in fully accepting his successor.

Could the power structure at Mega have implemented its
change program without the assistance of OD? Possibly, because
of Tom Rice's strong leadership, but the change process likely
would have taken much longer, been more difficult, and concluded with less satisfying results. Rice did not know the industry well enough to formulate a new corporate strategy, and his

senior executives had divided opinions on the existing strategy. Moreover, he would likely have encountered substantial resistance in trying to change both the entire organization structure and the executives who filled key positions. He was not aware of an educational process and conceptual format for bringing his executives together to address a logical sequence in major change topics — strategy to structure to positions to leadership — that proved crucial in stimulating and reinforcing events as they rapidly unfolded. Without OD, Rice would probably have had to rely, as many senior executives do, on a gradual and piecemeal series of forced minor decisions and compromises for negotiating his way through a political mine field. In doing so, he would have left many people feeling manipulated into accepting a situation that lacked coherence and commitment, thereby breeding further misunderstanding and political intrigue.

Politics at the Top

Would the OD process used at Mega work in all organizations in need of transformation? Clearly not. Certain critical conditions were present before the consultant ever arrived at Mega. There was a new CEO with a strong desire to lead, and the organization was in a high slack state in search of low slack methods. The CEO had already begun a collaborative effort that produced short-term results. Thus, a favorable situation existed that was at least partly receptive and susceptible to strategic change.

Any OD consultant, upon entering an organization, should make a careful diagnosis of the political dynamics at the top, especially when the issue is large-scale change. The change process ultimately hinges on collective leadership that shares a collective vision.

Unfortunately, there is little in the power literature to help us to understand these dynamics at the top. For example, Mintzberg (1983) argues that the CEO is "inevitably the single most powerful individual in the whole system of power in and around the organization." But this bold assertion is questionable in light of today's Pluralistic/Political organizations. A CEO's key subordinates may also have a strong power base, or there may be a strong chairman above the CEO, as was the case at Mega.

Our experience with top management groups reveals that the exercise of power is more reciprocal than allowed for in Mintzberg's assertion — I am influenced by you if you have control over something I want, but the extent of my compliance will be affected by my having control over something you want — giving credence to the old adage, "You scratch my back and I'll scratch yours." At Mega, the CEO obviously wanted a new strategic plan for the company, but he could not achieve it without the cooperation and knowledge of his key subordinates. Hence, he sought ways to reward and include them in a process in which they had a say over what happened to them.

Not all CEOs are as comfortable and effective at exercising power as was Tom Rice. We saw in Chapter 6 that some leaders have different needs for power and they may feel ambivalent toward using it even when they have it. They may try to win on minor issues while using up a "chip" that could be more valuable later on a major issue. Or they may not be sufficiently self-aware of their power bases and the power strategies that flow from these bases.

As a result, we see differences in the balance of power that emerges in companies over time between a CEO and his or her subordinates. They gradually test each other on various issues and learn the extent to which the CEO is willing to assert influence, and the extent to which they are willing to accept this influence. This contest of wills gives rise to at least four different political resolutions in a top group, as depicted in Figure 11–1 (Greiner, 1986):

Into which box did the Mega group fit? Before Tom Rice arrived, they were in a state of *covert resistance*. The former CEO had tried to exercise influence but his subordinates were unwilling to accept it. They strongly disliked the CEO who dictated decisions and played each subordinate against the other. They, in turn, threw up a protective barrier around each of their separate functional departments. This destructive dynamic was broken by the arrival and actions of Tom Rice. He treated the members with respect, and he rewarded them for using collaboration to achieve

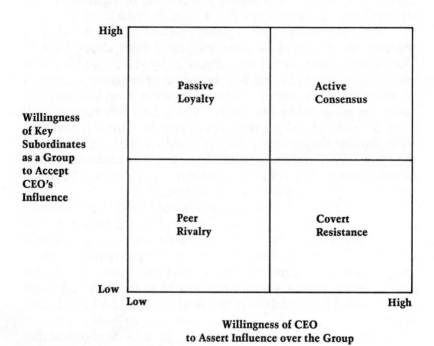

Figure 11-1
Political Resolutions in Top Management

short-term results. The OD process built upon this preestablished direction in moving the group toward *active consensus* on longer term issues.

The other boxes are also worthy of consideration because the OD consultant will confront them as well. Let us first understand the behavior of each political type, then we will discuss varying intervention strategies to apply in each case. Although we discuss these situations in terms of the top management of the company, it is likely they also apply to the apex of subunits in an organization, such as in a division or plant top group.

Peer rivalry is common when the CEO is unwilling to exercise influence. The CEO may have tried but found a lack of response, and so retreated. Other times, the CEO may be more interested in external affairs, such as dealing with the board of directors or participating in community activities. The resulting power vacuum is filled by rivalrous subordinates pursuing their own self-interests. Their power strategies are geared to competing for resources and rewards for themselves or their departments.

The upper-left quadrant, *passive loyalty*, also involves an inactive CEO, but here the subordinates are willing to follow if influence is exercised. We have observed this situation in companies in which a beloved founder retains control but refuses to manage the company. Key subordinates remain loyal to a CEO who acted as a mentor to them early in their careers and selected them for their current jobs.

Covert resistance is a dangerous situation in which a game of win–lose is being played out with the CEO. The CEO is trying to move an unmovable object: the subordinates have banded together in a coalition to obstruct the CEO. Such behavior emerges frequently in professional partnerships where the managing director runs afoul of powerful partners. It can also happen in a situation of peer rivalry, when a CEO reasserts himself and drives the rivals into banding together as an opposing coalition.

A seeming ideal is *active consensus*, a situation in which everyone is united and moving together as a team. But it can also be a case of "mass suicide" when the group is wrong in its assumptions about the market reality they are facing. A misguided team can go on making buggy whips when the horseless carriage is just around the corner. Nevertheless, powerful signals are given off by an integrated team to the rest of the organization, for good and bad. Fortunately, at Mega the top group analyzed correctly that there was still room to grow in their traditional market.

Intervention Approaches

OD consultants are presented with different challenges when faced with each of the four political dynamics described above.

The first consulting task is to place the client group in its appropriate box, and, more specifically, to determine how deeply mired it is in that box. Sometimes a group is verging on active consensus, which makes it easier for OD to have an impact, as was the case at Mega after Tom Rice arrived. But when the group is stuck in a deep pattern of covert resistance, it is unlikely to be moved by such OD techniques as team building or confrontation-meetings. The more distant the group is from "active consensus," the more complicated and difficult the intervention task is.

The second task for the OD consultant is to identify the basic issues that divide and attract the group within its box. Here we make a distinction between emotionally based self-oriented issues and substantively based work-related issues; the former is reflected in mistrust and personal animosity, and the latter in differences of opinion about such business topics as customer service. If subordinates deeply dislike their boss, as was the case at Mega before Tom Rice arrived, it makes little sense to focus an intervention on substantive work-related issues. However, when honest disagreements exist about the marketplace under a respected CEO, as was the case at Mega after Rice arrived, the intervention should concern itself with this substantive problem.

Often times, emotional and substantive issues are mixed together, which requires that the consultant sort things out. On a surface level, the group may be arguing about business issues, when underneath they simply do not trust each other. Alternatively, emotional feelings can be revealed in an honest disagreement about a business problem. The resulting interventions should be aimed at the dominant issue. For example, mild anger over a dominant business issue can be dissipated by focusing on specific areas of substantive disagreement, not on the anger itself. Conversely, in the Mega case, when Andy Davis opposed the creation of a new marketing department, his motivation was an emotional one, rooted in retaining power over the largest group in the company. Yet he cloaked this argument by saying that, "Marketing is already being taken care of in my group, which is the closest to the customer." His opposition could not be resolved at a logical level of business discussion. Instead, it required a private conversation with the CEO who "made it very personal. I said that I would do anything he wanted to make the job work."

Each box also provides clues about who the primary client

should be and how active the consultant must be. In the passive loyalty situation, a strong relationship needs to be built with the CEO and an effort made to persuade him or her to take action. Loyal subordinates are likely to follow the CEO's lead. The dynamics of peer rivalry often require a relationship with the most powerful peer who can step forward to lead his or her colleagues. In active consensus the client can probably be any member of the team, since that member will likely have the support of the entire team.

When deep emotional and substantive differences divide a group from its leader, as in covert resistance, this impasse will likely be broken only by eliminating the coalition. If the consultant has power with the CEO and the CEO is judged to be capable, then the first intervention is either to remove members of the coalition or to form a new coalition between the CEO and one or two of the most vulnerable resisters. If the consultant's client is one of the covert resisters and the consultant's power with the CEO is weak, it is probably time to leave gracefully before becoming a victim oneself.

For a consultant/change agent to be influential in these treacherous waters of top management politics, he or she must be astute in acquiring power and using it effectively. That is the subject of our last chapter.

12

Acquiring and Using Power as a Change Agent

In this concluding chapter, we return full circle to Chapter 1 where we asked the reader to examine his or her personal attitudes toward the use of power. Power cannot be separated from the personal qualities of the change agent, who must also want to acquire power and use it effectively and responsibly.

The OD consultant, whether coming from outside or inside the organization, encounters a different set of power issues from those normally facing a line manager.[1] Position power is not such an important factor because of the fleeting nature of projects; each stage in the change process requires new and different applications of power by the consultant. The type of power that it takes to gain access to key executives is not the same type of power that will later persuade these same executives to implement change.

There is no room for a messianic complex in a consultant's approach to power. Deluding oneself to believe that he or she will be embraced as the savior of an organization or that humanistic

---

[1]We use the terms *change agent* and *OD consultant* interchangeably, meaning a person with OD expertise who is seeking to be of assistance to management in moving an organization through a change process.

ideals espoused by OD will charm the organization into submission is fantasyworld stuff. The realistic consultant will recognize the need to win over powerful allies in the organization, and even then he or she will be tested at every turn.

The astute consultant can acquire sensitive information that yields tremendous power, but the unsuspecting consultant can be easily dismissed by a disgruntled senior executive who controls the purse strings. The naive consultant can also be abused by the organization's power structure. It is not uncommon for consultants to discover late in a project that they have been used to attain the hidden wishes of a senior executive; moreover, these wishes may have little to do with preserving human dignity in the organization.

Abuse of power by the change agent can also occur, sometimes unwittingly. Confidential information can be unintentionally released to the wrong people, and cause unintended harm. Or the consultant may become too powerful by usurping the role of line managers.

Types of Consultant Power

The change agent usually earns and re-earns power by helping the organization to move forward at each difficult hurdle. The effective consultant learns not to rely on any single power base or power strategy, but, instead, to be alert to the various types of power that are called for by the changing dynamics of an evolving situation. A variety of consultant power strategies is called for from the beginning to the end of the consulting process.

Access Strategies

No change project is possible without first gaining access to senior decision makers. Getting in the door depends mainly on one's reputational power base, composed of educational background, a track record of past accomplishments, experience in the client's industry, and the status of the consultant's employing organization.

Rarely is the consultant present to describe verbally these credentials to the hiring executives; instead, he or she must rely on a sponsoring executive to communicate this information to other client executives. The effective consultant is skilled in preparing materials (e.g., brochures, vitae, sample articles authored by the consultant) that create a favorable impression.

In addition to a reputational power base, the consultant will likely have to pursue a power strategy of *using social networks* to get his credentials in front of the sponsoring executive. Most client contacts come through personal references given by an established network of friends and satisfied clients.

In the Mega case, the CEO, Tom Rice, had known the consultant for a long time, beginning as an M.B.A. student. Later, the consultant assisted Rice in locating a position with a management consulting firm and worked with him on several projects. Rice not only respected the consultant but felt a close rapport with him. He became both the sponsoring and hiring executive.

Sales Strategies

Once in direct contact with key decision makers, the consultant needs more than reputational power to secure a client's agreement to proceed further. The client will scrutinize the consultant for other characteristics of a personality power base rooted in professional credibility and charisma. An assessment of personal chemistry takes place to determine if the consultant fits with the culture and is someone who they would like to work with on the project.

The consultant cannot passively sit back and wait for the client to make a judgment. Active listening by the consultant permits a restatement of the issues to test if the client has been accurately heard. Reciting examples from prior projects serves to lend assurance that the consultant indeed knows what he or she is talking about. Finally, the consultant must be ready with a proposed series of next steps should the client wish to proceed.

Using data from the initial interviews, a written proposal can be prepared that captures the essence of the client's concerns and serves as a basis for contractual understanding. An effective proposal will outline the project in terms that are understandable to the client, and at a cost that seems worth the added value being promised. Its underlying power strategy is to focus on needs of the target group. If the consultant proposes a project that seems unrelated to the problem or if the project is to be conducted in a way that does not fit with the client's working style, it will be rejected.

In the Mega example, although the CEO had confidence in the consultant, it was not clear if his other senior executives felt the same way. Hence, the consultant met them through personal interviews, not only to know them better, but to ask about business issues of concern to them. Informal feedback from them to Rice indicated that they were sufficiently impressed by the consultant's knowledge and personality power to proceed.

Diagnostic Strategies

The consultant needs the ability to dig deeply into the client's perceived problem and come back with data that he or she presents in ways that capture the client's attention.

Here the consultant draws on an expertise power base while building a new information base. A *playing it straight* power strategy is used. During interviews, the consultant must appear objective and trustworthy. The data are then analyzed to reveal significant insights that the client would not have been able to discover alone. And these insights must be presented in tactful ways that do not alienate important power holders.

At Mega, the consultant used interview data to design the agenda for the first retreat. These data were synthesized and reduced to a few major topics, and then were reviewed with the CEO so he could add his input. At the retreat, the consultant asked the group if these issues were indeed the ones they wished to discuss and focus on. They agreed, though with some uncertainty about whether progress could be made in solving them. The consultant relied on the twin power strategies of using data to convince others and focusing on needs of the target group.

Design Strategies

Power derived from insight into a client's problem is likely to create client dependence on the consultant, leading to heightened expectations for the consultant to propose ways out of the dilemma. The client will lose confidence if the consultant cannot provide assistance in arriving at a workable action plan.

Drawing upon a power base of expertise and information,

the effective change agent will need to propose at least tentative design steps that the client can react to and offer suggestions for consideration. Such steps have to be tailor-made in specific terms to fit the client's situation, not textbook generalities that leave the client up in the air.

Rarely will the client be persuaded by logic and data alone. A power base of charisma is usually necessary in order to give a presentation that elicits confidence that the consultant knows what he or she is talking about. It is necessary, too, in overcoming objections and answering difficult questions. Access to the key decision maker may be required to obtain approval at this critical point, especially if lower level executives are hesitant about whether or not to implement changes.

At Mega, the consultant already had and further cemented a close working relationship with the CEO. Together they designed the structure of the retreats, at which the CEO delegated responsibility to the consultant for moderating the discussions. At the first Mega retreat and throughout the project, the consultant and his assistant were frequently called upon to provide spontaneous outside knowledge that was relevant to the discussion. They also gave brief lectures to enlighten the discussion, such as presenting a conceptual framework for analyzing Mega's marketplace. In doing so, they were careful to use business terminology and examples that fit within the client's frame of reference.

Change Strategies

It is tempting for the OD consultant to become caught up in the expertise side of power, when, in fact, no change agent can possess all of the answers, and clients know this. Instead, the consultant will gain and use personality power through demonstrating sensitivity to the tone and momentum of the unfolding process.

Many occasions will arise when the change agent must intervene skillfully to move the discussion ahead. Conflicts will emerge that, if left untended, will set the project back. Sometimes these interventions must deal with issues of content where additional knowledge is needed, while other interventions serve to open up the discussion for those who may be silent resisters.

Much later on in the Mega project, at the third retreat when the group had grown tense over deciding which key executive should fill the operations job, the consultant turned to the CEO and said, "Perhaps we should take a break here and think about it before dinner, if that makes sense to you, Tom?" The CEO responded affirmatively, after which he took a walk with Andy Davis, who felt threatened by a proposed action that he perceived would take power away from him. The consultant set up this opportunity by intervening in a way that did not usurp power; instead, he deferred to the power of the CEO in recognizing that only Tom Rice, not the group, had to address the issue in a private setting.

Withdrawal Strategies

As a change project moves forward, the consultant must begin to transfer responsibility to others for managing the project and seeing it through to a conclusion. The change agent needs to help in creating power for others.

In the beginning stages of a change project, all eyes are on the consultant, many of them skeptical. But as the consultant responds effectively and gains power, too much dependence can be placed on the consultant. Therefore, the astute change agent will gradually help to organize other executives in taking on the project as their own. It may be a project task force that guides the project or it may be a particular manager who wants to lead an experiment in his or her segment of the organization.

Ironically, the change agent gains power from this transfer because he or she has empowered others who may feel grateful but somewhat puzzled about how to proceed. Here the consultant must be supportive but careful not to jump in with too much assistance and thereby undermine the new leaders. At the fourth Mega retreat, the consultant proposed that the group translate their discussion of growth, profitability, and culture change into three major programs, each headed by one member of the group. Volunteers immediately spoke up and the group proceeded to decide who would be best for which program. The leader of each program, not the consultant, then led a discussion of suggested steps to move the program ahead.

Substitutes for Power

Rarely does the OD consultant possess all of the power bases and strategies enumerated above. Furthermore, a consultant's power style may not be sufficiently flexible to respond to changing requirements. Therefore, one's lack of power must be supplemented by the power of others.

Broker

One approach is to act as a broker in securing the services of a more powerful consultant. As an internal consultant who may be short on reputation and charisma for selling power, one can go outside to find an experienced consultant with strong credentials, and then team up with that person in approaching top management. In essence, an alliance is formed with an outsider, who is probably drawn from the internal consultant's social network.

Sponsor

Another way to gain power is to develop political access with a powerful sponsor inside the organization. That key person can support the consultant initially in selling the project, and then the change agent can take over from there. The CEO at Mega carried such strong weight in sponsoring the outside consultant that his subordinates would have had to raise a storm of objection to prevent at least a first meeting with the consultant.

Pairing Up

As an external consultant, it often helps to pair up with another consultant who provides power attributes that you are lacking. In the Mega case, the original consultant brought in an assistant who possessed expertise power around strategic planning. Not only can another colleague provide complementary power bases and strategies, but two heads can be more objective than one.

Client Resources

A consultant with strength in personality power for process consulting but lacking in business expertise should tap the knowledge and experience of senior executives in a series of retreats or discussion meetings. This was the case at Mega, where the top management already possessed a great deal of knowledge about their industry and several had advanced degrees from business schools. They probably would have resented a consultant who attempted to dominate them in information or tradition power.

Self-Development

Substitutes for power, however, will carry a change agent only so far. The self-aware consultant will continually seek ways of enhancing and rounding out his or her personal power. For example, if one lacks educational credentials, reputational power can grow from the successful performance of several smaller projects. Certain selling skills, such as proposal writing, are easily learned through short seminars. Interviewing and intervention skills can be acquired and practiced in social settings outside a consulting engagement. Political access with potential sponsors can be cultivated through social and work contacts in nonconsulting environments.

Abuses of Power

The OD consultant is not just a powerful instrument for causing change. He or she must understand that serious moral and ethical responsibilities are also involved. Major changes affect the lives of many people, and usually thousands of dollars are at stake. The OD change agent carries a special moral responsibility because of the values inherent in the OD field itself. As mentioned in Chapter 1, there is an implied imperative for OD to take the *high road* in upholding and advancing the dignity and growth of people during the change process.

Powerful consultants can cause great harm, even unintentionally. Managers in the client organization can be intimidated by a too powerful consultant, conforming to the change agent's wishes even when they have serious reservations. Based on our experience, let us describe a few of the common abuses of power that we ourselves have fallen into or seen in the behavior of other OD consultants.

Broken Confidences

Interviews that probe into the hidden concerns of various managers, yielding information power, have to be carefully protected. In one situation, we revealed to a senior manager the content of a respected subordinate's interview, hoping that the weight of the comment would convince the senior manager about the existence of a serious problem. Two hours later the subordinate was called in and severely criticized by the senior manager. In another instance, two consultants carried on a casual conversation on an elevator about sensitive material revealed to them by the CEO, only to learn later that they had been overheard by an attorney who was a close social friend of the CEO.

Claiming Credit

The powerful consultant can easily fall into the trap of self-oriented power behavior, attributing credit to oneself for the brilliant insight that broke a logjam in the client's boardroom. Although it may be true, self-aggrandizement only undermines the power of client executives. One consultant we know was dismissed from an engagement for giving a speech to fellow consultants in which he discussed how he was "straightening out a Fortune 100 company," which he mentioned by name. Effective OD consultants learn to bestow appropriate public credit on their clients, not themselves.

Taking Over

Often times the change agent will become frustrated with client executives who are hesitant to act. The temptation arises to fill the void with an expertise power base and a persistence power strategy. One of us once took the floor from the head of a project planning task force, and started giving directions to other members of the committee. Members of the committee looked confused, staring back at their appointed leader to see if he agreed. Later, the consultant apologized to the leader and discussed how he could give more constructive assistance from the sidelines.

Manipulation

The OD consultant often favors certain behavioral techniques that he or she has used successfully in prior situations. Such techniques are tempting to repeat, if only to serve as a means for demonstrating one's expertise power. Unfortunately, the consultant may force such techniques on a situation where they do not apply. We have seen several consultants push organizations into large-scale training programs designed by and featuring the consultant as the star performer.

Walking Away

Instead of skillfully transferring power to the client, consultants can leave prematurely, causing the client to flounder, still needing help. Only half the job is done by arousing the client to take action through a brilliant diagnosis. To leave without offering assistance on implementation steps can leave the client confused about what to do next. A resentful client will not be a good referral.

Being Abused

Consultants depend on clients for their welfare, but this can lead to pleasing the client at all costs. Losing a contract can damage a consultant's ego as well as his or her pocketbook. Thus, instead of seeking to acquire power and use it constructively, the insecure consultant becomes a servant to the existing power structure.

One reputable management consulting firm with which we are familiar had a $500,000 contract with a major bank. The senior consultant on the project met the chairman of the bank by accident at the airport and offered him a ride into town. When the chairman inquired about the project, the consultant revealed that the bank would not meet its budgeted profit goal for the quarter. The chairman was surprised and, upon returning to his office, called in the president to ask for an explanation. An angry president, who had hired the consultants, then returned to his office, called the consulting firm, and asked that the senior consultant be removed from the project. The consulting firm agreed to the request, explaining later to the senior consultant that even though he was right, the project was too important to lose. The senior consultant accepted this reasoning and took an assignment on another project.

Acquiesence by the change agent to client requests that are not in the best interests of the organization only serves to undermine the consultant's power for future effectiveness. In the above example at the bank, the consulting firm never recovered. They continued to be used in a deceptive self-oriented power strategy by the president, whose real motive was to build a case for removing the chairman. Both the president and chairman eventually lost their jobs when bank performance deteriorated and the bank was taken over.

In such blatant cases, the change agent should obviously refuse to comply. The consulting firm had sufficient power in relation to the bank president because he was dependent upon them for their final report, which he hoped would show the chairman to be incompetent. If the president still insisted on dismissing the senior consultant, the consulting firm could approach the chairman and seek him as their client sponsor. If the chairman then backs off, there comes a time in every consultant's career to walk away from a job.

Often times the OD consultant slips into the role of servant without being aware of it. Instead of maintaining objectivity and integrity, the change agent gradually identifies with the viewpoint of a few key power holders, especially those who are supportive of the consultant's ideas. As a consequence, the change agent isolates himself from others with less power who may have important contributions to make toward the program. Resentment toward the consultant builds at lower levels and his or her effectiveness is diminished.

An important reason why a change agent should acquire his or her own power base is the maintenance of personal integrity. This permits not only an independent relationship with the key power holders, but also allows one to uphold the views of those with less power. The success of any large-scale change project depends eventually on the reactions of people many levels removed from top management.

Sense of Self and Situation

This book has argued for the OD change agent to develop increased sensitivity to the power dynamics existing in a client organization. Yet, to confuse sensitivity with compliance runs the risk of becoming a puppet for the existing power brokers. The effective consultant also needs to acquire power to act as a strong counterweight to those powerholders who prefer the past and to those who would run over people.

Thus, the OD change agent needs not only to assess outwardly the power dynamics in the organization, but he or she must be self-aware in acquiring and using power appropriately and responsibly. A strong sense of power in oneself is essential, including one's limits, strengths, and attitudes toward the use of power. Increased knowledge of power in both the situation and oneself will greatly enhance one's ability to assist others in changing while also preserving integrity for all those involved. That is the challenge in seeking the *high road* to power and organization development.

Bibliography

Adorno, T. W., E. Frenkel-Brunswick, D. J. Levinson and R. N. Sanford. 1950. *The Authoritarian Personality.* New York: Harper & Row.

Argyris, C. 1962. *Interpersonal Competence and Organizational Effectiveness.* Homewood, Ill.: Irvin-Dorsey.

Auletta, Ken. 1986. *Greed and Glory on Wall Street.* New York: Random House.

Baldridge, J. V. 1971. *Power and Conflict in the University.* New York: John Wiley.

Bennis, Warren. 1969. *Organization Development.* Reading, Mass.: Addison-Wesley.

Bennis, W., and B. Nanus. 1985. *Leaders.* New York: Harper & Row.

Blake, Robert R., and Jane Mouton. 1964. *The Managerial Grid.* Houston: Gulf Publishing.

Burns, T., and G. M. Stalker. 1961. *The Management of Innovation.* London: Tavistock.

Christie, R., and F. Geis. 1970. *Studies in Machiavellianism.* New York: Academic Press.

Crozier, M. 1963. *The Bureaucratic Phenomenon.* Chicago: University of Chicago Press.

Cummin, P. C. 1967. "TAT Correlates of Executive Performance." *Journal of Applied Psychology* 51: 78–81.

Cyert, Richar M., and James G. March. 1964. *A Behavioral Theory of the Firm.* Englewood Cliffs, N.J.: Prentice-Hall.

Dalton, M. 1959. *Men Who Manage.* New York: John Wiley.

French, J. R. P., and B. Raven. 1959. "The Bases of Social Power." In *Studies in Social Power,* edited by D. Cartwright. Ann Arbor: University of Michigan, Institute for Social Research, pp. 150–167.

Friedlander, F., and L. D. Brown. 1974. "Organization Development." *Annual Review of Psychology,* Vol. 25, 313–341.

Gabarro, John J., and John P. Kotter. 1980. "Managing Your Boss." *Harvard Business Review* Jan–Feb: 92–100.

Galbraith, Jay. 1979. *Designing Complex Organizations.* Reading, Mass.: Addison-Wesley.

Greiner, Larry E. 1983. "Senior Executives as Strategic Actors." *New Management,* Vol. 1, No. 2, 13.

Greiner, Larry E. 1986. "Top Management Politics and Organizational Change." In *Executive Power,* edited by S. Srivastva et al. San Francisco: Jossey-Bass, pp. 155–177.

Greiner, Larry E. 1980. "OD Values and the Bottom Line," In *Trends and Issues in OD: Current Theory and Practice,* edited by W. Burke and L. Goodstein. La Jolla, Ca.: University Associates, pp. 319–349.

Greiner, Larry E., and Virginia E. Schein. 1981. "The Paradox of Managing a Project Oriented Matrix: Establishing Coherence within Chaos." *Sloan Management Review,* Winter, 17–22.

Hickson, D. J., C. A. Lee, R. E. Schneck, and J. M. Pennings. 1971. "A Strategic Contingency Theory of Intraorganizational Power." *Administrative Science Quarterly* 16, 216–229.

Kearns, Doris. 1976. "Lyndon Johnson's Political Personality." *Political Science Quarterly* 51 (3), 385–407.

Kets de Vries, M. F. R., and D. Miller. 1984. *The Neurotic Organization.* San Francisco: Jossey-Bass.

182   *Power and Organization Development*

Kipnis, D., S. M. Schmidt, and I. Wilkinson. 1980. "Intraorganizational Influence Tactics: Exploration in Getting One's Way." *Journal of Applied Psychology* 65, 440–452.

Kotter, John P. 1986. "Why Power and Influence Issues Are at the Very Core of Executive Work." In *Executive Power*, edited by S. Srivastva Assoc. San Francisco: Jossey-Bass, pp. 20–32.

Kotter, John P. 1985. *Power and Influence*. New York: The Free Press.

Kotter, John P. 1979. *Power in Management*. New York: Amacom.

Kotter, John P. 1977. "Power, Dependence and Effective Management." *Harvard Business Review*, July–August, 125–136.

Lawrence, Paul, and Jay Lorsch. 1967. *Organization and Environment*. Boston: Division of Research, Harvard Business School.

Lennerlof, L. 1967. "ITAT: Studies Performed with a Versity of TAT Intended for Use in Industrial Psychology." (Report # 49). Stockholm: Swedish Council for Personnel Administration.

Lorsch, Jay, and John Morse. 1974. *Organizations and Their Members: A Contingency Approach*. New York: Harper and Row.

Maccoby, Michael. 1976. *The Gamesman*. New York: Simon and Schuster.

Machiavelli, N. 1964. *The Prince* (T. G. Gregin, Ed.) New York: Appleton-Century-Crofts.

McClelland, D. C. 1975. *Power: The Inner Experience*. New York: Irvington.

McClelland, D. C., and D. H. Burnham. 1976. "Power is the Great Motivator." *Harvard Business Review*, March–April, 100–110.

Mintzberg, Henry. 1983. *Power in and Around Organizations*. Englewood Cliffs, N.J.: Prentice-Hall.

Mintzberg, Henry. 1978. "Patterns in Strategy Formation." Management Sciences 24 (9): 934–948.

Mintzberg, Henry. 1973. *The Nature of Managerial Work*. New York: Harper & Row.

Mirvis, P., and D. Berg, eds. 1977. *Failures in Organizational Development and Change*. New York: John Wiley.

Mohrman, S., and T. Cummings. 1987. "Self-Designing Organizations:

Towards Implementing Quality-of-Work-Life Innovations." To appear in *Research in Organizational Change and Development,* Vol. 1, edited by R. Woodman and W. Passmore. Greenwich, Conn.: JAI Press.

Naisbitt, John. 1982. *Megatrends.* New York: Warner.

Perrow, Charles. 1970. "Departmental Power and Perspective in Industrial Firms." In *Power in Organizations,* edited by Mayer N. Zald. Nashville, Tenn.: Vanderbilt University Press, pp. 59–89.

Peters, Thomas. 1986. *Passion for Excellence.* New York: McGraw-Hill.

Pettigrew, A. M. 1986. "Some Limits of Executive Power in Creating Strategic Change." In *Executive Power,* edited by S. Srivastva et al. San Francisco: Jossey-Bass, pp. 132–154.

Pettigrew, A. M. 1975. "Toward a Political Theory of Organization Intervention," *Human Relations, 28,* pp. 191–208.

Pfeffer, J. 1981. *Power in Organizations.* Marshfield, Mass.: Pitman.

Pfeffer, J. 1978. *Organizational Design.* Arlington Heights, Ill.: AHM Publishing Corporation.

Pfeffer, J., and G. R. Salancik. 1974. "Organizational Decision Making as a Political Process," *Administrative Science Quarterly, 19,* 135–151.

Porter, Michael. 1980. *Competitive Advantage.* New York: The Free Press.

Quinn, J. B. 1980. *Strategies for Change.* Homewood, Ill.: Richard D. Irwin.

Raven, B. H. 1965. "Social Influences and Power." In *Current Studies in Social Psychology,* edited by I. D. Stein and M. Fishbein. New York: Holt, Rinehart and Winston, pp. 371–382.

Sayles, L. R. 1964. *Managerial Behavior.* New York: McGraw Hill.

Schein, E. H. 1980. *Organizational Psychology.* Englewood Cliffs, N. J.: Prentice-Hall.

Schein, V. E. 1987. "Strategies Used by U.S. and U.K. Managers in External Relationships." Presented in Best Papers Proceedings, Annual Meeting of the Academy of Management, at New Orleans, Louisiana, August, pp. 220–223.

Schein, V. E. 1985. "Organizational Realities: The Politics of Change." In *Contemporary Organization Development,* edited by D. D. Warrick. Glenview, Ill.: Scott Foresman, pp. 86–97.

Schein, V. E. 1979. "Examining an Illusion: The Role of Deceptive Behaviors in Organizations." *Human Relations* 32 (4):287–295.

Schein, V. E. 1977a. "Individual Power and Political Behavior in Organizations: An Inadequately Explored Reality." *Academy of Management Review* (2): 64–72.

Schein, V. E. 1977b. "Political Strategies for Implementing Change." *Journal of Group and Organization Studies,* March: 42–48.

Schein, V. E., and L. E. Greiner. 1977. "Can Organization Development be Fine-Tuned to Bureaucracies?" *Organizational Dynamics,* Winter, 48–61.

Schlilit, W. K., and E. A. Locke. 1982. "A Study of Upward Influence." *Administrative Science Quarterly* 27: 304–316.

Strauss, G. 1962. "Tactics of Lateral Relationships: The Purchasing Agent." *Administrative Science Quarterly* 7: 161–186.

Winter, D. G. 1973. *The Power Motive.* New York: The Free Press.

Zaleznik, A. 1970. "Power and Politics in Organizational Life." *Harvard Business Review,* May–June, 47–60.

Zaleznik, A., and M. F. R. Kets de Vries. 1975. *Power and the Corporate Mind.* Boston: Houghton Mifflin.

Power and Organization Development
Larry E. Greiner and Virginia E. Schein

For too long, power and organization development have been juxtaposed as two opposing and contradictory approaches to management. *Power and Organization Development* argues that OD and power can and should be reconciled and integrated in the implementation of change. Power is essential for getting things done in an organization, for implementing ideas, obtaining budget approvals, dealing effectively with other departments, and promoting new policies and procedures. The purpose of this book is twofold: to provide the reader with a solid grounding in the role of power and politics in organizations, with a specific focus on how managers use power bases and strategies to get things done, and to provide the reader with strategies and intervention techniques for bringing about change in an organization.

Larry E. Greiner is professor of management and organization in the School of Business Administration at the University of Southern California. He is an internationally recognized scholar and consultant on the issues of organization growth, structure, and strategy. Dr. Greiner is author of the classic Harvard Business Review article, "Evolution and Revolution as Organizations Grow," as well as co-author of the book *Consulting to Management*. Dr. Greiner holds D.B.A. and M.B.A. degrees from Harvard Business School and a B.S. from the University of Kansas. He has previously served on the faculties of the Harvard Business School, INSEAD in Fontainebleau, France, and the University of Kansas.

Virginia E. Schein has lectured extensively to management audiences on the subject of "Power and Politics," both in this country and in Europe. She is a former associate professor of management at the Wharton School and is currently an organizational psychologist and consultant to business and industry in human resource management. She received a Ph.D. in industrial psychology from New York University and graduated cum laude from Cornell University.

Today this state-of-the-art series, edited by Beckhard and Schein, has been expanded to include 20 titles by authors such as Dyer, Gerstein, Harris and Porras, with many new titles planned for the future. It has grown to represent many distinct facets of OD, covering various organizational areas and technologies. Diversity and innovation are still at the heart of this series and the unifying characteristic of the series is the ability of these outstanding authors to define and broaden the meaning of organization development.

Addison-Wesley Publishing Company   ISBN 0-201-12185-9

9 780201 121858